Twin Killing:
The Bill Mazeroski Story

by John T. Bird

Photography Credits

AP/Wide World Photos . . . . *Front Cover, 111, 182, 224*

Bettmann Archive *5, 65, 132, 159, 206*

George Brace. . . . . *Frontispiece, 2, 14, 38, 52, 70, 80, 102, 116, 128, 240, 252*

Mazeroski family collection. *256, 257*

National Baseball Library
and Archive
Cooperstown, N.Y. *5, 65, 76, 87, 132, 159, 206, 245*

Philadelphia Phillies *124*

Pittsburgh Pirates *8, 18, 24, 31, 49, 56, 60, 89, 92, 97, 125, 140, 146, 152, 166, 172, 174, 175, 178, 188, 194, 200, 212, 217, 220, 230, 258, 259, 263, 265, 266, 269, 270, 272, 273, 276, 278, 280, 281, 282, 286, 289, 294, 295, 300, 316*

Pittsburgh Post-Gazette *28, 259, 262, 270, 271, 292, 295*

Milo Stewart . . . . *Back Cover*

Harry Walker collection *235, 304, 310, 313*

For Susan

Acknowledgments

Special thanks to Sally O'Leary of the Pittsburgh Pirates front office (rookie year, 1964, retirement date, 1996); her advice was invaluable. Bill Guilfoile and the other professionals at the National Baseball Hall of Fame and Museum made my research trip to Cooperstown pleasant and productive.

Many thanks also to my literary agent, Maryanne Colas, Manhattan's most ardent Maz fan; *Twin Killing's* interior page designer, Jane McGriff Herlong; Barry Mitchell, who designed the cover; and Curtis Ralya and John E. Davis III, for providing technical support.

Bill Mazeroski's friend since childhood, business agent Bill DelVecchio, was instrumental in making *Twin Killing* a reality, as was Milene Mazeroski, Maz's wife. And to Bill Mazeroski, who with twenty-two other talented gentlemen cooperated with me to produce this unique record of the Mazeroski era, my deepest thanks. It was a true pleasure.

Table of Contents

Introduction

A twin killing, in baseball parlance, is a double play, and Bill Mazeroski is the greatest pivot man to ever turn a double play. No other second baseman has approached his records for double plays in one season (161 in 1966), or in a career (1,706). A seven-time All-Star who won eight Gold Gloves, Bill is the greatest fielder to ever play second base; he is possibly baseball's best fielder, period.

Twin Killing: The Bill Mazeroski Story is an authorized oral history of Bill Mazeroski's career with the Pittsburgh Pirates, which spanned 17 seasons from 1956 to 1972. It is the anecdotal judgment of twenty-three players who witnessed Maz's greatness at various stages of his career. In 1994 I interviewed all these players (including Maz) in person, and edited their taped reminiscences.

Twenty recollections are from former Pirates. Only lifetime Yankee Bobby Richardson (who played against Maz in the 1960 World Series), Manager Harry Walker, and Coach Alex Grammas never played for Pittsburgh.

The chapters are grouped by position, and run in roughly chronological order within each position. The only vacancy is right field, which Roberto Clemente patrolled with brilliance over Maz's entire career. (Clemente died on a mission of mercy to Nicaragua in 1972.)

A source of inspiration for this biography is Lawrence Ritter's *The Glory of Their Times*, a pioneering oral history of baseball against which all others are measured. Ritter's preface addressed the issue of ghostwriting players' reflections: "This is their story, told in their own way, and in their own words." That neatly describes the recollections of the twenty-three players in *Twin Killing*, who offer expert insights on Mazeroski, baseball, and themselves. Since my editing for clarity was a matter of subtraction, not addition, this book is most assuredly the words of these players.

Before I started interviewing players, I felt strongly that Bill Mazeroski should be in baseball's Hall of Fame, by virtue of his superb statistical record (see Epilogue). I finished *Twin Killing* convinced that two intangible qualities, Bill's character and his value as a teammate, only add to the luster of his marvelous accomplishments on the diamond. Bill is eligible for induction into the Hall of Fame by a Veterans Committee vote in March, 1996.

As I began my interviews, Alex Grammas, Maz's old third base coach, boldly predicted that I could travel all over the country, talk to folks in any state, and not hear one bad word about Bill Mazeroski. Alex was right. Bill Mazeroski was an exceptional ballplayer who happens to be a very fine fellow. Pull up a chair and listen to his story.

On the Field with Maz: 1956-1972

■ Portion of career spent as teammate of
Pirate second baseman Bill Mazeroski

▨ Rest of career

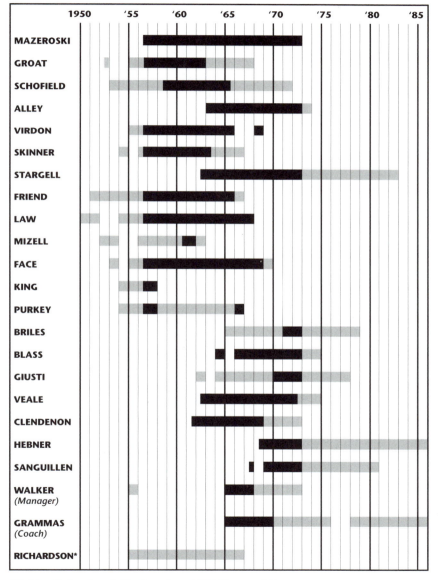

*Bobby Richardson's Yankees faced Bill Mazeroski's
Pirates in the 1960 World Series.*

"I always said my wife could have led the league in double plays with Mazeroski at second base if she were a shortstop. He was that good."

– Dick Groat

1

Dick Groat

Dick Groat was not blessed with speed; quickness and a knack for positioning made him one of the top shortstops of his generation. The College Basketball Player of the Year at Duke University in 1952, and a two-time All-American in baseball, Dick played for the Fort Wayne Pistons of the National Basketball Association before casting his lot with his hometown team, the Pittsburgh Pirates. A fine hitter with a lifetime average of .286 – superb for a shortstop – Groat was the National League M.V.P. in 1960, leading the major leagues in hitting with a .325 average as captain of the World Champion Pirates. Traded to St. Louis after the 1962 season, Dick responded with his best year, hitting .319 with a league-high 43 doubles. An All-Star with the Pirates in 1959, 1960, and 1962, and with the Cardinals in 1963 and 1964, Groat's specialty was advancing baserunners via the hit-and-run. Dick was part of two exceptional double play combinations, teaming first with Bill Mazeroski, then Julian Javier. After contributing to another World Series triumph, with the Cardinals in 1964, Groat finished with short stints with the Phillies and Giants. Dick owns and operates Champion Lakes Golf Course close to Ligonier, Pennsylvania, and announces University of Pittsburgh basketball games.

Everybody remembers Maz for the home run. I remember Maz as the greatest second baseman that ever played the game. I sincerely believe that. Not just that he turned a double play better than anybody else ever turned it, but he had marvelous range; he had great instincts; he never threw to the wrong base; even his rookie year, his mistakes were so few and far between it was unreal. He's the greatest defensive second baseman in the history of the game of baseball.

My rookie year was '52; then I went in the service for two years. I played in '55, then Maz came up in '56. I would imagine I had at least ten or twelve second basemen in the two years prior to Maz coming up. And those weren't two full years, because I didn't sign until June.

My rookie year, I started with George Strickland, who was a shortstop and moved to second base. Clem Koshorek, Jack Merson, Johnny Berardino, Dick Smith, Spook Jacobs, Johnny O'Brien. At least ten. All with their own styles that you had to get used to. When Maz came up, that was the end of that game.

The Pirates made a deal in 1960 that solidified our hold on the pennant when they traded Julian Javier for "Vinegar Bend" Mizell. "Vinegar Bend" was 13-5 with us that year, a key factor in our winning. The Cardinals ended up with Julian Javier, the second-best second baseman I ever saw when I was traded to the Cardinals. How lucky can you be: I had Mazeroski from '56 through '62, then I had Javier in '63, '64, and '65 with the Cardinals. Had Javier not been traded to St. Louis, he'd have never been the second baseman at Pittsburgh. He would have never beaten out Mazeroski.

* * * * *

I had a father who always dreamed of having a son become a major league baseball player. In those days, there was no Little League baseball. You played on the playgrounds. I started to play when I was a freshman in high school. I played American Legion in high school, and then I was fortunate to gain a basketball scholarship to Duke

University. I wanted to go to Duke because it had great baseball and basketball programs.

An article in Sport magazine my senior year in high school, 1948, said they played big league baseball at Duke University. The story was about Coach Jack Coombs, who had been an excellent pitcher for the Philadelphia A's, playing for Connie Mack. Coach Coombs was a marvelous person in every way, a great teacher, a great coach.

I was an All-American as a junior and in my senior year, when I signed with the Pirates right from the College World Series.

I joined the Pirates the next day. Watched one game, pinch-hit the next game, then started every game the rest of the season. I was fortunate to lead the Pirates in hitting my rookie year. It was on-the-job training. I probably should have been in the minor leagues but it worked out well for me, going right to the big leagues.

I had always promised myself when I was a youngster I was going to go straight to the big leagues. I was lucky enough to do that, thanks to Branch Rickey.

"Straight to the big leagues...thanks to Branch Rickey"

I finished my season with the Pirates, and went back to Duke. I was only carrying ten credits because I was so close to graduating. I had a light schedule on Monday, Wednesday, and Friday.

And I played with the Fort Wayne Pistons in the N.B.A. They would fly me around in a private plane. I would go to class on Monday, then Tuesday morning, fly in to New York, play in Madison Square Garden, fly back, go to class on Wednesday, and fly in to Philadelphia. In those days, all the N.B.A. teams were in the East.

It worked out well. I thoroughly enjoyed the few games I played in the N.B.A., thirty-four, whatever. I played against Bob Cousy. I was a much better basketball player than I ever was a baseball player. I consider myself today a retired basketball player.

Over sixteen years playing baseball, including my two years in the service, I probably didn't get four leg hits a year. I could hit the ball deep in the hole and they'd still throw me out! I just didn't run that well. But if your first step or two are quick, nobody notices your lack of speed on a basketball court. God gave me the ability to put the ball in the hole. I could score. Plus I was a pretty good defensive player and ball handler. Whereas in baseball, I didn't have power and I didn't run well. It took me ten years, until I went to the Cardinals, to develop a very good arm. With those drawbacks, I never considered myself a great baseball player.

When I got out of the service and rejoined the Pirates for spring training in 1955, Bobby Clemente was a rookie – he was one marvelous athlete. There wasn't anything Bobby couldn't do on a baseball diamond. He had probably the most outstanding God-given talent I ever saw. He could run. He hit with power. He had a great body. Little thin waist, strong through the chest.

In those days the Pirates were not good, but there was enthusiasm, just being in the major leagues, trying to make yourself a better player, trying to learn the game.

The '60 World Champion team was Mr. Rickey's team. He had signed Mazeroski; he had drafted Clemente, ElRoy Face, Friend, Law, Skinner and me.

It took awhile to get ourselves organized. You don't know when a team is going to mature. Our General Manager, Joe Brown, made the deal for a pitcher, third baseman, and catcher, Haddix and Hoak and Burgess, which solidified everything. We didn't win it in '59, but we were a very good club that didn't make mistakes. We were not a power club, but our outfielders always kept the double play in order.

They would never miss cutoff men, and the infielders knew exactly what they were supposed to do. In the clubhouse meetings, Law was going to pitch one way, Friend another, and so forth. They pitched them that way. This is probably true for Maz, too: I know I became a much better infielder the better my pitching staff was. You're better because you're always in the right position.

If you ever sat in a dugout when Burdette and Spahn were pitching against you, you'd hear guys coming back saying, "Jesus, I can't hit the ball any harder. It was right at them." There's a reason it was right at them. That's the way they were going to pitch you, so that's the way the infielders played you. I didn't have great range. I had to know every hitter in the National League, how they would hit against Haddix, against Friend, against Law.

Shortstops I admired? Ernie Banks, obviously, because of his hitting ability. Maury Wills. Roy McMillan was a marvelous shortstop. A great defensive shortstop. Best hands of any shortstop in the National League.

When I was a kid, the two shortstops I looked up to the most were Alvin Dark and Pee Wee Reese. Both were a big help to me, especially Alvin Dark.

My rookie year, Alvin took me underneath the stands after a game with the Giants and gave me an education on making the double play at second base. I was getting my ankles all torn up; he spent about an hour with me.

Hell, I had all kinds of scars on my legs from hanging around second base. The infielders that come across second base now, they're all going to right field, because every time anyone gets on first base, it's, "Break up the double play." You just can't hang around second base. I wasn't very bright as a kid. Everybody was turning me upside down.

Maz had extremely strong legs. He would stay right there. The best way I can describe Mazeroski – having played short-stop alongside him for six years – is when the ground ball was hit, I'd just catch it, get rid of it, and Maz would do whatever had to be done. I've seen him take the ball off the short hop and turn it into a double play. No way anybody could compare with him turning the double play. Maz was just magnificent.

* * * * *

Dick Stuart at first base wasn't nearly as bad a fielder as everyone kidded, even though he was nicknamed "Dr. Strangeglove."

Dick's biggest problem defensively was his lack of concentration. Thinking about hitting instead of playing defense. It wasn't that his hands were so bad. Dick just wanted to hit the ball. He didn't want to be catching it or fighting ground balls.

Dick Stuart

To Dick, fielding was a necessary evil. He had to do it to get to the plate. But you couldn't help but love the guy; he was fun to be around, you enjoyed having him as a teammate.

L.A. Coliseum, 1959. We're playing Gil Hodges as a dead pull hitter. Hodges hits a line shot off to Don Hoak's left, one skip; Hoak goes over and it nicks the end of his glove. I catch it backhanded off Hoak's glove.

Stuart isn't paying any attention to the fact that I might have caught the ball. As soon as he sees it go off Hoak's glove, he turns his back to let Hodges turn first base. I catch the ball and as soon as I let it fly, there's a big number seven looking right at me. Dick's back is to me. I throw the ball right over first base, one hop in the stands.

When we get out of the inning and get back to the dugout, Stuart comes in all smiles, telling everyone, "Two-base error, E-6." And that's exactly what it was. Hodges would have been out by five, six steps.

Everybody makes errors. Physical errors are part of the game. The great managers, the Freddie Hutchinsons, the Danny Murtaughs, never say boo to you for a physical error. Mental errors, different story. As a professional baseball player, you're not supposed to make mental errors.

When you'd make the pivot, Maz always gave you the ball where you could handle it. Never got you killed at second base. So many little things Bill Mazeroski did better than any second baseman that ever played the game. We led the major leagues in double plays for five consecutive years. Then he and Alley broke the National League record for the most double plays made in a season. I always said my wife could have led the league in double plays with Mazeroski at second base if she were a shortstop. He was that good.

And positioning. When Maz was a kid, I had a couple of years' experience on him. I remember this vividly. If I would move Maz and tell him to play here or play there, I never had to tell him a second time, ever. He had great instincts. He'd remember hitters. Maz was the perfect second baseman for any shortstop that ever lived.

* * * * *

My biggest honor was not M.V.P. in 1960. It was getting more votes than any player in either league for the All-Star game in 1963. It was quite a compliment, after Joe Brown had traded me to St. Louis. That was when the players voted. It was no popularity contest. They know who's playing and who isn't. And overall, 1963 was the best year I ever had. Better than the '60 season.

In 1960, I broke my wrist on September 6th, and three weeks later, I pinch-hit on a Thursday night against Milwaukee, then started Saturday and Sunday, the last two games of the season before the World Series. Ducky Schofield had done a magnificent job at shortstop while I was out.

It did not hurt me to swing the bat as long as I swung at a strike. Swinging at a ball just a little bit out of the strike zone, I'd feel excruciating pain up my arm. But I was able to play in the '60 World Series, thank God.

The Yankees were a notorious high-ball hitting club and our pitching staff had a tough time getting the ball down. Bobby Richardson...we couldn't get the ball below his waist for love or money. Bobby set a World Series record with twelve RBI's.

On the young Pirates teams of the early '50s, Mr. Rickey used to sell us on the fact that great teams win one-run games; really bad clubs lose one-run games.

When the Yankees beat us badly in their Series victories – Ford shut us out twice, 10-0 and 12-0, and we lost 16-3 – there was no second-guessing. The game was over, that was it. But the Pirates were able to win every ballgame we had a chance to win in that Series.

Game 2 of the Series, they beat us 16-3. Danny Murtaugh had taken me out, so I could put my wrist in the whirlpool, and I didn't see the game, but when it was over, Virdon came around the corner with Maz. "Boy, Dick, you missed the granddaddy of all of them!" I said, "What are you talking about?" They said, "Mantle hit a ball over the iron gate that you would not believe. It's the hardest-hit ball we ever saw!"

Seventh game, Virdon's hit that got Kubek in the throat...I was in the on-deck circle. It really did take an ugly hop. The Forbes Field infield could get really chopped up; you'd get some bad hops out there.

* * * * *

A philosophy taught me by Mr. Rickey was you have to make yourself needed on the ball club. I didn't have power, so I had to learn to move the ball around to advance runners. With the tying run at second base, nobody out, you'd better get him to third base. That is the way the game should be played.

I couldn't walk up there and hit the ball out of the ballpark. So I worked at developing my ability to handle the bat. I was able to play in the major leagues over a sixteen-year period.

Getting traded was devastating. The Pirates felt Schofield could do the job at shortstop and they could get pitching in return for me. Don Cardwell came to the Pirates for me. I had grown up in Pittsburgh and I never wanted to play for anyone but the Pirates. But the three happiest years I ever spent in a baseball uniform were wearing the Cardinal uniform.

I enjoyed going back to St. Louis for the 30th reunion of the '64 World Championship club. There's something special about clubs that win pennants. It's a close relationship, a friendship you never lose. Like Virdon and Maz and Skinner: we're still very close friends and were all extremely hurt when Harvey Haddix died. You go through a pennant race – the '58 Pirates, the '60 Pirates, the '63 and '64 Cardinals – you're all experiencing the same worries, the same fears. It's something you never forget.

* * * * *

I always said I was the luckiest baseball player in the world. I went from Hoak and Mazeroski to Ken Boyer and Javier around me at third and second base. From Bill Virdon to Curt Flood in center field.

There's no reason in God's world Bill Mazeroski shouldn't be in the Hall of Fame. It's a disgrace that he isn't. Many sportswriters didn't have any concept of how great Maz was. "Oh, he hit a home run that won the World Series." That's bullshit. Mazeroski did everything on a baseball diamond.

I had a Pittsburgh sportswriter tell me that he voted for Luis Aparicio instead of Mazeroski! My comment at that time – I was as good as Aparicio. My lifetime batting average was .286; his was .262. I played on two World Championship teams, won an M.V.P., won a National League batting title. And I have no right being in the Hall of Fame. But I didn't play in New York or Chicago or L.A. and neither did Mazeroski.

Johnny Pesky had come to the Pirates from the Red Sox – he had played his whole career in the American League – and asked me about Mazeroski. I told him, "Nobody could have ever been better than Mazeroski at second base." Pesky said, "Dick, that's nice to hear you say, because I've coached with him for a few years and I feel exactly the same way, and I played my whole career in the American League."

Bill gave you a hundred and ten percent every single day he walked on the baseball diamond. Always in a good humor, great to have on a ball club, never second-guessed anybody. You couldn't ask for a better teammate.

Billy was very, very quiet. He led more by what he did on the field. He was not a holler guy. Maz led by example. If he was injured, it didn't make any difference; he still played.

When Bill's number was retired in 1987, I said a few words. I was quite nervous. At Three Rivers Stadium or any stadium, if you're not used to the acoustics, it's very difficult to maintain your concentration, because you say something and it comes out instants later. I did not know what I was going to say when I stood up. I was told it was a nice tribute. What I said came from the heart. I am very proud to have been part of that program honoring Bill Mazeroski. I am proud he is my friend.

"Maybe Bill didn't hit as much as most guys in the Hall of Fame. But they didn't play second base like Bill did."

– Dick Schofield

2

Dick Schofield

Dick "Ducky" Schofield broke in as an 18-year-old "bonus baby" with the Cardinals in 1953; he was traded to Pittsburgh in 1958. Dick was a key figure in the Pirate stretch run in 1960, filling in brilliantly for an injured Dick Groat. Schofield succeeded Groat at shortstop in '63 and '64. Traded to the Giants in 1965, Dick led National League shortstops with a .981 fielding percentage. In 1966 Dick played for the Giants, Yankees, and Dodgers; in 1968 he played in his second World Series, with St. Louis. After spending '69 and '70 with the Red Sox, Dick split his nineteenth and final season with the Cardinals and Brewers. A lifetime .227 hitter, Dick could play second base, third base, or shortstop. His son, also named Dick, has gone "Ducky" one better by leading each league in fielding percentage as a shortstop. "Ducky" Schofield lives in Springfield, Illinois.

My father played in the minor leagues. Wilkes-Barre, Pennsylvania, here in Springfield, Illinois, over in Joplin and Kansas City, Missouri. He played eleven years.

He spent a lot of time with me. Hit me a lot of ground balls. I give him the credit. He taught me how to play.

I always played shortstop, even as a kid. Later in the big leagues, I played a lot of second base and third base. I was the very first bonus baby for the St. Louis Cardinals back in 1953. I don't think anybody knew my name or cared when I joined the Cardinals. But I was treated well, I'll have to say. I roomed with Alex Grammas. We've been friends for a long, long time. Alex was a super infielder; he could play shortstop. And I remember I was in complete awe of Stan Musial. Stan was always good to me. As a bonus baby, with only sixteen teams in those days, you had to take the place of a guy on the roster who belonged in the big leagues, where you didn't belong.

I played part of '55 and part of '56 in the minors at Omaha. Then I came back to St. Louis in '57.

I was traded to Pittsburgh in 1958. That was the first time I really got to know Maz. I knew who he was. Everybody would talk about how he could make the pivot on the double play better than anybody who had ever played second base. Maz had fantastic hands. He made every play look very easy. He just caught the ball and threw you out. It wasn't fancy.

On balls hit up the middle, Maz had a natural sidearm or underhand throw; he had a great arm from behind second base. He threw a lot of guys out at first base after catching the ball going into center field. Other guys had to jump and do all kinds of things to throw the ball; Bill's natural arm motion let him get a lot on the ball. Maz was no speed merchant but he got a good jump on the ball and made all the plays.

He was an intelligent player who played hitters well. To me, Maz was as good a second baseman as anybody that's ever played. Maz's instincts were excellent. His first step was superb. Like Brooks Robinson. Brooks couldn't run a lick, but he could go to his left or to his right as quickly as anybody.

Maz could catch a ball and get it to the first baseman

quicker than anybody that ever played the game. That's why he made so many double plays. Dick Groat and Gene Alley could play, too. That helped a bit.

I played two years every day with Maz and I didn't worry. Just get the ball to him. That simple.

You can't teach what he had: his reactions, the unique way he did things. The good Lord gave him these abilities.

And when runners would slide into him, they weren't hitting a little body. Maz was a pretty good-sized man and a strong fellow. Never saw him really get hit hard.

1960 was the first time I was on a team that won the pennant and then the World Series. It's the best year I can remember in baseball. My teammates were good players and outstanding people.

Mizell came over from the Cardinals for Javier – "Vinegar Bend" was 13-5 with the Pirates. If I remember right, he beat the Giants four or five times.

Javier was a second baseman: with Maz around, he wasn't going to play at Pittsburgh. He went to St. Louis and became a great player. So the trade was a break for him and a break for the Pirates and Mizell.

We beat Cincinnati two times that season in the ninth inning. We had two outs and I think we scored seven runs in the top of the ninth inning. Bob Skinner hit an inside-the-park home run to win the game. We won a ton of games from the seventh inning on. Having ElRoy Face didn't hurt. He was a fantastic relief pitcher.

Clemente and Groat and Hoak and Law had outstanding years. Bill Virdon played center field as well as anybody ever played it.

On that team, Maz and I were always good friends. His roommate, Virdon, too. Joe Gibbon was my roommate and good friend while we played with the Pirates – about six years. I was close to Harvey Haddix, Mizell, Skinner...Dick Stuart was a great guy. There was a lot of agitation on that club: guys would get all over each other. We had fun.

Bill Virdon and Haddix and their wives and my wife were always good friends as were the Laws, the Friends, Maz and Milene. The wives were close on that team.

I went to San Francisco in '65. I didn't want to leave Pittsburgh, but it was the best thing for me. San Francisco was very cold and windy. Whoever built Candlestick Park made a mistake – it's not a very good place to play. I'd envy visiting teams that only had to be there three days.

I led the league in fielding percentage there one year, but that's because the infield was much better than Forbes Field's – not as many divots. These days the fields are manicured. I think the Players Union had a lot to do with that.

When I played at San Francisco, the infield was fantastic. The grass was so thick, batters couldn't hit the ball through the infield, so you could get to a lot more balls. It was tough for me at the plate; I was a singles hitter.

The toughest play for me in the field was the ball hit to my right, in the hole, where you've got to plant your foot and throw the guy out at first base.

Dick Schofield with wife Donna, daughters Kim and Tami, and future Gold Glove shortstop Dick Jr.

I enjoy watching Ozzie Smith play. I put him in a category with Maz. You can only play shortstop so well. But Ozzie's not quite the same infielder he was three or four years ago. You know, I've got a son who's a pretty good shortstop. I don't think anybody plays shortstop any better now.

I hurt my arm with the Giants, and couldn't throw. They sold me to the Yankees, I ran around the outfield chasing balls, and my arm still bothered me.

I went to the Dodgers in September, 1966. Played third base every day and did fine. I think I had something to do with the Dodgers winning the pennant. I was signed one day late to be eligible for the post-season, which was a disappointment. But you're going to have some in the game. I can't complain too much. I was pretty lucky.

Sandy Koufax in 1966 was awesome. I didn't need a glove to play third. Guys just did not hit the ball. Sandy pitched like Bob Gibson pitched in '68 for the Cardinals. I was on that Cardinals team.

They had won the Series in '67. That '68 team was probably the best I ever played on. We lost the '68 Series to Detroit in seven games. We should have won, but didn't.

I went to the Red Sox for two years, coming back to the Cardinals again in '71. Then they traded Jose Cardenal and me to Milwaukee. I finished the last half of the year out in Milwaukee. The next year Dave Bristol, the manager, told me he wanted me to be his utility player. Frank Lane, the General Manager, told me if Bristol wanted me, that was fine, but if I didn't want to play, I could manage San Antonio in the Texas League.

I went to spring training. Lane called me in and told me he was going to release me. Here I am left high and dry. In those days, that's the way things worked. I didn't get the job as manager in the Texas League and I came home.

Pittsburgh called me three or four times to manage in the minor leagues after that. But you just didn't make any money, and my kids were getting older. My oldest girl, Kim, was excelling in track; she went to the Olympic trials. My other girl, Tami, was growing up and was active in sports; Dick was starting Little League baseball, so I decided to stay home. I'm still here. I'm kind of glad I came home.

When Dick was twelve years old, he was twice as good as the other kids. He knew how to play, because I taught him how. I never made him do it. Never said, "Okay, today at 4pm, we're going to go out and do this and stay out until 6pm." My Dad, same thing. He never made me do anything.

Dick makes all the plays. He's led the American League in fielding four times. He plays a lot like Maz. That's a pretty good guy to be like.

Maz making the double play was textbook. He'd take some throws that would be terrible and still turn the double play. Spectacular was the norm for him.

Dick Stuart at first base was a different story. I'd catch the ball and throw it to Maz; when Maz threw it to Dick, the question was: Is Dick going to catch it? But Dick took all that in stride. Everybody liked Dick – but he did have trouble with that leather thing.

Maz was unassuming. And reliable. You knew he would be there to play, even if he was hurt. He was, and is, a family man. I remember him always being with his wife. He's a good guy you can't help but like.

* * * * *

One highlight for me was getting to play shortstop one evening in Milwaukee in 1959. The greatest game ever pitched. The scoreboard was off to my left where I could glance at it – every time I'd look, it showed two strikes, no balls, and two outs. Seemed like every Brave who walked up there had two strikes. We had twelve hits and didn't score a run. I led off, had three hits, and never scored. Harvey Haddix was perfect for 12 innings before losing in the 13th, but Burdette pitched pretty well, too.

Of course, there's the seventh game of the '60 World Series. Maz has said many times he wasn't trying to hit a home run. In Forbes Field, it wasn't that easy. That was a pretty good poke to left center field. It happened so quickly. All of a sudden you're at home plate jumping up and down. You couldn't pick out a more deserving guy than Maz to hit that home run.

Another highlight is the first game I was ever in. I went in as a pinch-runner in Chicago, with the Cardinals in 1953. Roy Smalley was the Cubs' shortstop. By the time I got off the field I was wringing wet. Smalley and Bob Ramazzotti, the second baseman, were hollering at me, "Get back! Steal! Slide!" I was in a nervous sweat when I got back to the dugout. I didn't get picked off, so I must have been standing on first base.

And I remember the first hit that I got, in Brooklyn, off Johnny Podres. That was my first time up.

Odd things stick in your mind, too – like deliberately sticking my thumb in a lemon. In 1960, I used to always warm up before games with Bob Skinner. Once I threw a ball to Skinner and Hal Smith reached in; Hal caught the ball and threw me a knuckle ball, just screwing around. I went to catch the ball and it missed my glove – you know how a knuckle ball darts – and hit me square on the end of my thumb. Blood came shooting out of my thumb like ink from a pen. I thought I'd broken my thumb.

I didn't say anything to anybody. Between innings I stuck it in ice water. The next day was an off day. Somebody told me to buy a lemon, cut the center out, put the lemon over my thumb, then tape it. I slept all night with that lemon on my thumb and I kept it on the next day, all taped up.

That thumb got about twice the size it should have been. I threw the ball with three fingers for a while because I couldn't hardly use my thumb. After a couple of weeks, it was still sore, but it had gotten better. Maybe the lemon helped!

People ask, "What was your biggest thrill in baseball?" I tell you what, putting the uniform on and walking on the field, I think that's a thrill. That was what I'd wanted to do since I was a little kid.

I have a hard time believing Ryne Sandberg, making seven million dollars a year and quitting, in the middle of the season. I don't understand that. I'm not too sure somebody would have done that back when we played.

*   *   *   *   *

Baseball's still the best game. There's no clock. You've got to get three outs an inning. It's that simple. You can't stall; you've got to get them out.

Look at the Texas Rangers. A lot of hitting, the pitching is a little shaky, the defense is too, therefore they struggle. You don't win 9-8 every day because you're not going to score nine runs every day – good pitching is going to get you out. In any sport, if you've got that good defense, it keeps you close enough to give you a chance to win.

When the Yankees had great teams in the early '60s, they could play defense. Bobby Richardson at second base, Clete Boyer at third. Maris and Mantle in the outfield. Elston Howard. They had defense, not just good pitching and hitting. You've got to be able to catch the ball, you know.

Bill Mazeroski could catch the ball. Maybe Bill didn't hit as much as most guys in the Hall of Fame. But they didn't play second base like Bill did.

*"**W**henever we were playing, I was always hoping they would hit it to Maz."*

– Gene Alley

3

Gene Alley

From 1964 to 1969, Gene Alley teamed with Bill Mazeroski to form a record-setting double play combination. In 1966, when the Pirates set a National League record of 215 double plays, Alley was in on 128. Gene had very good range, a fine arm, and sure hands. Since he played most of his home games on the difficult infield of Forbes Field, Gene's career fielding percentage of .970 is impressive. Named to the National League All-Star team in 1967 and 1968, Gene played with the Pirates for a decade, retiring after the 1973 season. Gene is now in the printing business in his hometown of Richmond, Virginia.

M az never really caught the ball, never really closed his glove over it, turning the double play. He could tilt his glove at an angle and hold his hand just so. It was a wonder the ball stayed in there – then it would slide out in his hand just like that. He was the only one I saw do it like that. I tell you he could field a ground ball. I remember the first time I saw him, the first time I went to spring training with the Pirates. I was 20 years old. I watched him taking ground balls and I thought, man, if you have to be this good to be in the major leagues, I'll never make it. He was really great. It was fun just to watch him field ground balls. Never saw him make a play that looked hard. Everything looked easy. I know from taking ground balls, that they're not all easy. Maz could do it and make it look like it was nothing.

* * * * *

I did play with the Richmond Optimist's Club, but we did not have Little League when I was coming up, mostly just choosing up sides and playing, that's what we would do in the summer. I pitched, played third some. I didn't play shortstop much until high school. In high school or Little League, they use the guys who have a good arm and try to make them into pitchers. I wasn't a pitcher, I just threw hard.

I signed out of high school in 1959. Russell Rowe, one of the Pirates' bird dogs, recommended me. I had tryouts with the White Sox, Yankees and other teams, but the Pirates showed the most interest.

I loved baseball when I was little. I was probably like most other kids – I followed baseball. The Yankees were my favorites. Phil Rizzuto, guys like that. Just watching them play Saturday afternoon games on TV, that was a big thing then.

I played five years in the minors, working from D ball up to Triple A, then got called up to the majors in '63. I went to Iowa, North Dakota, two years in Asheville, North Carolina, then Triple A in Columbus, Ohio.

I played my first year at shortstop and then had trouble

with my arm. The next year, they moved me to third. The following year they moved me to second base. I played two years at second base. All of a sudden, they wanted to see me playing short again. Sent me to the Arizona Instructional League for two years, but out there they moved me around everywhere too. They told me, if you play more positions, it makes you more valuable, with a better chance to make it to the majors. So I would play second one day, one day third, move all around. Then all of a sudden in 1963 I went to Triple A; they stuck me at shortstop. Honestly, I wasn't ready to play shortstop at the Triple A level. I hadn't played the position much since high school.

At shortstop you've got to be ready for everything. You never know what's going to happen, you've got to go all over, go back, come in, make the double play, anything. It's a pressure position.

* * * * *

First game in the majors? I was called up, the team was in Milwaukee and I played that night against the Braves; Warren Spahn was the pitcher. September of '63. I grounded out three times that night. I was surprised because I thought that he'd throw a lot harder than he did. Never gave you anything to hit. Screwballs away, curveballs down and in.

You have to feel that you belong in the majors; when you start playing against guys, and you have their baseball cards, it takes a little while to get used to that. You need time to adjust. I had had a chance to go to spring training with Dick Groat and also Dick Schofield. I'd watch how they made plays, how they fielded ground balls, where they played in certain situations. You learn a little bit from everyone you watch. Groat was a positional shortstop, knew how to play the hitters. When I saw him, he didn't cover that much ground, but was always in the right spot. Like Cal Ripken. Ripken seems to be in the right spot all the time.

* * * * *

I don't really remember the first time I met Bill Mazeroski. It had to be the first year, when I was 20 years old going to spring training. You go out and you take ground balls together. We used to play golf and fish together at spring training. Maz would always be fishing way down in the bay somewhere. Though I can't remember the first double play we turned together, once we played together a few years, it seemed like fans would come out just to see if we could turn double plays. It was fun.

"Spring training...Maz would always be fishing"

Maz had quick feet. You can't throw the ball unless your feet are planted. That's what made him so quick. That's why it looked like he had such quick hands. He was quick with his hands, but he was quicker on his feet – that's what made him stand out.

Today, most players don't realize how lucky they are. The money they make. I didn't make good money. I've got to admit one thing about today's players, they're bigger and stronger than we were! We weren't allowed to lift weights, which has a lot to do with hitting more home runs and playing longer.

Back in my day we didn't make enough money to not work in the winter time. You tried to keep your weight down, but in the off-season you went to work to make enough money to get through the winter.

* * * * *

I liked the infield at Forbes Field when they put a little water on it, it was soft, it was good. When they didn't water it, it was like a road. Hard as a rock. It was difficult, like two infields. When it was watered, the dirt stayed together, it was smooth, nice, but when it got hot in the summer and it didn't have water on it, the sun baked it; your spikes wouldn't even go in the dirt, it was so hard. I liked playing on grass better than on Astroturf because I grew up playing on grass, I learned how to play on it. When they came out with Astroturf there was no more circling balls; it was more of a side, back, sideways thing. It just changed the way shortstops played the game. We'd play deeper, going side to side.

Pickoffs? That wasn't a big thing for the Pirates. The main thing was to do it once in a while; scouts would see you use it and write up that you'd try to pick off runners.

The contact play, man on third base, say, one out and the infield's up and suddenly you have a ball that's hit to you not too sharply: you've got to figure out in a split second whether to go home or not. You either end up looking good or looking bad. You know the guy who's on, how fast he is, how hard the ball was hit and you can see him breaking, so you know whether you've got a shot. Usually if the guy's hit it kind of hard, you've got a shot. Unless the baserunner's off and running with the pitch. That's a judgment. Most infielders know who's fast, who's not, who's a good baserunner, who's not. Once you've played against a guy, you should know all those things about him. I could watch a guy hit once or twice, and I'd know how to play him.

Lou Brock and Maury Wills were the key base stealers I played against. Some guys would try to catch you off guard. They wouldn't try to steal that often but they could steal. Mays didn't try to steal all the time. I don't think he wanted to take all that banging on his legs.

Relays are essential. There is a place for every player on every ball that's hit. After you play awhile, you know where you have to go, where you should be on every play. That's just like somebody at any job, knowing where to be all the time. If there is a guy on first base and the ball is hit down the left field line, you know you're supposed to go to a certain spot. If the ball is hit to right field...it's knowing where you're supposed to be. The main thing is just knowing how to play. Like base-running mistakes. Stealing third with two outs, guy gets thrown out. What's the reason? Unless you can walk over there, why are you even going?

When Maz and I were playing, guys stayed in the minor leagues four or five years, and really learned how to play the game. If they got to the major leagues, they knew all that stuff. Our manager, Danny Murtaugh, told us all he was going to do is pick the Pirates lineup; all we were going to do is go out and play. Murtaugh figured we were major leaguers, we should know how to play baseball.

I played with Maz mostly in '65, '66, and '67. Then I hurt my shoulder in '67 and was in and out a lot in '68 and '69. Then Maz hurt his legs, in '68 or '69. After that we really did not play together a whole lot.

What stands out about Maz? Well, he never missed the ball, for one thing! I don't think I ever saw him make many errors and he never missed many balls at all. In 1966 we screwed up two double plays the whole year that we should have made; Maz had 161 that year, which is still the major

Alley and Maz turn two – the Pirates' 215 double plays in 1966 is still the National League record

league record. Nobody else is close.

Maz was not the type of person who was real flashy, who would stand on his head to make a play. He just gets the guy out and makes it look so easy that you don't notice, you don't appreciate what he does, until the end of the year when he's set records.

Just playing with him and knowing that he was going to do his job made me realize that I was going to have to hold up my end of the bargain. That put a lot of pressure on me, because he did everything so easily. If a ball was hit that I could not reach, people would say, you've got to catch these balls – Maz can catch them. I would try to tell them, I wasn't as good as he was!

Maz just went out and played. He didn't say much, and we didn't say much. Even though we worked together we didn't talk a whole lot. He was easy to be around. If a play came up, I knew where he was going to be. I didn't have to guess. And he knew if he caught the ball that I would be right where I was supposed to be, at second. Balls hit up the middle, he'd come up with the backhand catch, but if he didn't have any chance of throwing the guy out, he would flip the ball to me and I would throw the ball to first base. Once we had the guy out but the first baseman dropped the ball. The first baseman was so surprised because he saw Maz catch the ball, running away, and didn't see Maz flip the ball to me, because I was coming around behind Maz, throwing the ball from another angle. We did that about two times and he dropped the ball. We finally did it in Atlanta. That's just knowing. Maz knew where I was and Maz knew what he was going to do with the ball.

When you room with somebody, you know how he feels. In a lot of games, guys would slide into Maz, try to take him out of a double play. He always had cuts and bruises on his legs, shins. He probably didn't play a game when he didn't have something wrong with his legs.

Maz and I knew how to play the hitters. We would play them according to how the pitcher was supposed to pitch 'em. If the pitcher didn't pitch the way we went over in the pre-game meeting, then we were out of position. We would rely on the pitcher to pitch to hitters the way he'd said he would. You don't want to play down the middle anticipating hard stuff away and then get change-ups. You'd hear people say, well, he's out of position. But it's really that the pitcher is not pitching the way he said he was going to, and you can't be moving during the pitch. I watch this on television. The announcers will see an infielder move right before the pitch and say, oh, he's doing a good job, he's moving. He knows they're going to throw a breaking ball. You can give pitches away like that. A hitter sees somebody move over there and he knows. That's a no-no. You don't do that. Maybe kick the dirt before the pitcher throws, but you don't move once the catcher has given the sign.

* * * * *

The feed to Maz on the double play was easy. He used to tell me where he did or didn't like it. If you'd throw the ball with a lot of speed or over his head, it would make it a lot harder. Usually you would just try to hit him where he liked it. All you had to do was just come close.

Maz would get to the bag, be almost stopped, then let the ball tell him where he was going to go. That's the way you should make the double play. You should never be running for the bag full speed: if the guy makes a bad throw, you can't catch the ball. First of all, you've got to stop, and you might have to move sideways. So the best thing is when the ball is hit, you get to the bag and you almost stop, you see where the throw is and then you go ahead. You don't know if you're going to have to catch the ball back here, or whether it's up here. Maz always got to the bag, kind of stopped, saw the ball, where it was going to be, then went ahead and made the pivot.

His legs were big and strong, and his first step to the bag was quick. Pete Rose came down one day, trying to break up a double play; Maz had caught the ball and stepped to throw. Pete did one of those side blocks and just slid down him. It was like somebody trying to do a body block against a tree.

I don't think I ever saw anybody take him out who hurt

him. Lots of guys hit him because many times the ball wasn't hit that hard, and even though it was a hit and run, you're still trying to get a double play. I guess Maz was lucky that he didn't get hurt more at second, because it doesn't take but one time for somebody to hit you wrong on the side of your knee.

It's up to the baserunner to get down when you're throwing to first. That's one of your defenses. You throw the ball right at his head. You're coming across making a double play as if nobody is coming down there. You throw it and if the baserunner wants to stand up and get hit in the head, that's up to him. I've seen a lot of guys get hit in the helmet. Most will get out of the way. Another reason why Maz didn't get hurt on slides as much is how he threw the ball; he'd jump, get in the air. Once you're in the air and somebody hits you, he can't hurt you. Once Maz had thrown the ball, he would do a little hop. They didn't catch Maz with his feet planted, which is when runners will hurt you.

Maz used a very small glove. We used smaller gloves then. The infielder gloves today, most of them, are huge. But Bill's glove...they wouldn't even use it in Little League today. If a Little Leaguer saw Maz's glove, he would say, man, that glove is too small! Throw that thing away.

I used about one glove a year in games. I had two gloves all the time: one being broken in during practices, one to use in games.

* * * * *

A Houston Astro, John Bateman, said that every time somebody was on first and he hit a ground ball at us, there wasn't any point in running because he knew it was going to be a double play. If you can make the double play other teams respect that. I think pitchers appreciate guys like Maz more than anyone else. They know with one out if they are going to walk somebody, in one pitch they could get out of the inning. Back in the dugout. If you can't turn the double play, that means you've got to face another hitter; give a team another chance, usually you end up in trouble. How many times have you seen a pop fly drop, you don't throw them out, how many times right after that have you seen a hit? It happens a lot.

My favorite double play? Ronnie Brand hit into it at Houston. Last inning, I think the bases were loaded and one out and Ronnie hit a ground ball in the hole at short. When the play was over there were three guys lying on the ground; me, Maz and Clendenon. Everybody ended up on the ground. Ronnie, when I saw him later, said there was no way there to get a double play; I said, blame Maz for that. I will always remember that play.

My highlights included playing in the All-Star game, but playing on the 1971 Pirate team that won the World Championship has to be the biggest thrill of my whole career. There is nothing like that. Playing with Clemente was a big thrill for me. I liked him. He really was hard to get to know, but once you got to know him, he was fun to be around.

Anything to get him mad – if we got him mad, Roberto would go out and get three or four hits! We would tie his socks in knots. I don't know if you ever noticed Clemente when he came on the field before the game, he was always fixing his pants or his buttons. He couldn't find his uniform, we would hide it or tie it in knots. He would always wait until the last minute to get dressed, go get his uniform, and his socks would be tied in knots. There weren't too many people that had the talent Roberto had.

Willie Stargell could play. We came to spring training the first year together in the minor leagues in '59. I didn't play with him the first year, he played in one Class D league and I went to another, but the next year we played together in Grand Forks. I was a third baseman. He was a tall and skinny center fielder. I led that team in home runs with Willie Stargell on the team!

The next year, he started getting big in Asheville, started putting on weight and getting stronger and started hitting home runs.

The last two years Maz played, '71 and '72, it was kind of sad. An era was over. That was what hit me the most. You hate to see a long, great career like that come to an end. But Maz was the same as he ever was. He didn't change. I don't think he liked not being able to play much. Just sitting around as a utility player, he wasn't cut out for that.

Looking back at all the years I played with Bill, I remember his double plays, but I cannot picture him missing a ball. I couldn't tell you one time that I remember him making an error. I know he made some. It's crazy, but I cannot recall Maz missing a ball. Maz was the best second baseman that I saw while I was playing. I don't know if there is anybody better today, either.

Maz was like a country boy coming in to play a city game and doing it in the country way. Quietly getting the job done, doing it without a lot of fanfare. Maz didn't want the spotlight, he just wanted to play, and be the best he could. I don't think anybody has ever done it better. If the game was on the line, you'd want to look over there and see Maz at second base. Whenever we were playing, I was always hoping they would hit it to Maz.

"The impressive thing about Maz was that he did everything perfectly at second base. I backed him up for ten years and never got a ball."

– Bill Virdon

4

Bill Virdon

Rookie of the Year with the Cardinals in 1955, Bill hit .319 and finished second to Hank Aaron for the 1956 National League batting title. Flanked by Bob Skinner and Roberto Clemente, Bill anchored the longest-running outfield trio in baseball history, together from 1956 until Skinner was traded in 1963. Winner of the Gold Glove in 1962, Virdon patrolled spacious Forbes Field with speed and grace. His most notable hit was the bad-hop grounder in Game 7 of the 1960 World Series that caught Yankee shortstop Tony Kubek flush in the throat; most likely a tiny pebble turned Virdon's routine double play ball into the catalyst of a Pirate comeback. Today Bill is bench coach for the Pirates.

I was born in Hazel Park, Michigan. Moved to Missouri and went to high school in West Plains, a small town 100 miles from where I live now in Springfield, Missouri. I was a Detroit Tigers fan. I followed the Cardinals, admired Musial, but one particular player I followed was Hank Greenberg of the Tigers. What did he have, 58 homers one year, 183 RBI's one year? I never saw him play much, four or five games, but I listened to a lot of games on the radio. That was early on in the broadcasting of games on radio, back in the late '30s and '40s.

I always enjoyed playing baseball, but Missouri high schools had very little baseball; I played football three years in high school. I played a little bit of baseball during the summertime on town teams. We'd play here and there.

Following my junior year in high school, a friend had gone to a tryout camp and they recommended he go out to Kansas and play amateur ball for the summer, fifty, sixty ballgames. I talked him into taking me with him. The club I played with was affiliated with the Yankees, made up of college players. I was between my junior and senior years in high school the first year I went. My friend and I went out; I made the club and he didn't. I stayed that summer, went back following my senior year, was scouted and that's how I got into baseball. Tom Greenwade scouted me and sent me to a tryout camp of Yankees-scouted players in Branson, Missouri, today's country and western capital. There were 1500 people in that little lake town, mostly fishermen. I signed and went to Independence, Kansas, D ball, in 1950. I jumped to Norfolk, Virginia the next year, B ball; I skipped C ball. The next year I went to Binghamton, New York, A ball, and then I split a season between Kansas City, Missouri, and Birmingham, Alabama, which was Double A.

Following that year I was traded from the Yankees to the Cardinals and spent a year in Rochester, New York, Triple A. So I spent five years in the minor leagues. I had a good year in Rochester and broke in with the Cardinals in 1955. Played that year in St. Louis and the following year, May 17th I believe, I was traded to the Pittsburgh Pirates – a few weeks after I got there, Maz got there. Of course he played longer than I did. And I played almost ten years with the Pirates and a year with the Cardinals.

* * * * *

Getting traded from the Yankees, where Mickey Mantle played center field, was the best thing that ever happened to my major league career. Mantle signed as a shortstop and I signed as a center fielder, so that wasn't an initial concern. When I went to Branson, first tryout camp, Mantle was with Joplin, Missouri and everybody was talking about how good he was going to be. I was thinking to myself, not knowing about the major leagues, if all the major leaguers are like Mantle, I am in trouble, because his talent just stuck out head and shoulders above everybody else's!

The main enjoyment in my business is winning, and the first year in St. Louis we finished 7th or 8th and with Pittsburgh, 8th the first year and 7th or so the second year. It was disappointing that we weren't winning, but I was playing in the big leagues, holding my own the first couple of years, maturing.

I played in the outfield with Roberto Clemente all ten years I played with Pittsburgh. Usually a center fielder will call off the other fielder on a catchable ball but with Clemente on your side, you don't get carried away with that. And you'd know Roberto would be there if you were not able to get it.

Only once in ten years did we have a problem communicating. Once in the 1960 World Series, the fans were so loud, screaming so much, that we ran together. I caught the ball, though I had to peek to see if I had it in my glove. We could not hear each other.

Other than that, we knew where each other was all the time. That was with a lot of ground to cover, too. But Roberto never tried to convert me to the basket catch. I caught the way I could catch best and he caught it like he liked to catch it. He didn't drop any, so nobody argued with him.

Best center fielders I saw? Willie Mays – probably the best all-around player I've ever seen. Duke Snider was a fine center fielder with the Dodgers. Billy Bruton with Milwaukee. Richie Ashburn, Philadelphia. Of course Curt Flood. I'm sure I'm missing somebody I should be talking about.

Comparing notes with those guys? Back in my day, that wasn't done. Unless you happened to be friends with somebody from the home town, or you'd played with somebody. You might go out and eat with him. We didn't fraternize too much.

What you learn on your own, after you get up here, about the players you're playing against, is where they hit the ball, how they hit it off different pitchers. It's the experience you gain, knowing how to play and where to play, that makes you a better outfielder. Positioning is important, but that usually comes from the coaching staff. They have charts now. They just started doing that at the end of my career. We did it from observation. You watch your pitchers pitch against the batters. You learn where batters hit the ball most of the time. You play percentages. It's like Maz playing second base. It never looked like he was in the wrong place.

Not only was Maz good at reading the hitters and how the pitchers were pitching to them, but his instincts were great, his movements were good and when he caught the ball he threw them out; so positioning had something to do with it. If you have a pitching staff that throws fly balls all the time, your second baseman is not going to get many chances. If they keep the ball on the ground, he's going to get a good bit more. A great deal of those balls that Maz got to were outs because he knew where to play, but a lot of it was the pitching staff. They wanted the hitters to hit the ball on the ground to second base, because they knew Mazeroski would catch it.

How many of Maz's 1,706 double plays did I see? Almost all of them. I only missed about two years. I played with him for ten. I managed for two years in the Mets organization and I came back to Pittsburgh as a coach, then managed the Pirates for a year. I had a good vantage point in center for ten years.

If the batter hit the ball with any kind of authority to the other infielders, it was a double play. There was no doubt for anybody on the Pirates or anybody in the National League.

When Maz got the ball on the pivot of the double play, out at first. Maz could get it to first quicker than anybody I've ever seen. I've seen a lot of good ones, but nobody could turn a double play like he could. Maz was the best because he did not have to have the good throw to make the double play. He could take it from any position.

Take the throw from third, short, first, he could take it from any position, high or low, and get rid of it from that position. A lot of infielders want the ball right here in the chest so they can handle it. If the ball is not right there, they have to reach for it, they have to come back to get it, so no double play, but Maz could take it up here and get rid of it, take it down here and get rid of it and that's why he was so effective. He could still get velocity on the ball to the first baseman to complete the double play.

* * * * *

The good fielding second basemen I saw...Jackie Robinson was pretty good, and a couple of years was all I saw him play. Javier was one of the better ones. He came in later on about the last four or five years of my career. Junior Gilliam was not bad with the Dodgers after Robinson. But Maz saved so many runs and he saved so many hits from going through.

The fans enjoyed Mazeroski in Pittsburgh. But I think the big fan appeal is offense, running the bases, hitting base hits. There is a lack of attention given to defense.

Memorable plays in the field...the best play that I remember making, I didn't make. It turned out all right, yet I didn't make the play. That was a ball off the left center wall in Forbes Field. There were vines on that wall, heavy vines. Andre Rodgers hit the ball, we were winning 1-0, in 1960. Two outs and he hit a ball high to the wall. I had a lot of time to run and I saw it was going to hit right at the wall or on the wall. I saw I couldn't catch it on the ground so I ran and put my foot in the vines, grabbed the vines and went up to get the ball.

I didn't get up quickly enough and didn't quite get my glove turned around to where I could catch it. The ball bounced down into the ivy and I went right with it. If it had not been for the ivy, the umpire would probably have called Rodgers out. But I couldn't get the ball out of the vines without falling down. The ball kept falling down and I kept going down with it as I'm hanging on the vine and I ended up coming out with it on the ground. I looked around. Vinnie Smith, the umpire, had come out and had seen what had happened. Vinnie was right on the scene and as I turned around he's making the safe call. I immediately went to him to see whether he had followed me down or not. Well, everybody in the ballpark, except for Vinnie Smith and me, thought I'd caught the ball and they were screaming and hollering. Andre Rodgers, influenced by the reaction of the fans, thought I had caught it. He rounded second and trotted towards third. I threw the ball to third base and he was tagged out! So a play that I didn't make was my most memorable one.

As for stealing a home run, catching a ball that's over the wall, things were a bit different back then. There weren't too many fences that had padding, and few that you could climb. A lot of them were 18 to 20 feet high. In San Francisco they had the storm fence. You could climb that.

Candlestick Park was probably the toughest park to play in because of the combination of wind and sun. The wind was not true, it didn't blow one way all the time so you'd know how to play, it was a swirl. You'd read the ball off the bat and then the wind would play tricks with it.

In any park, I think the toughest play is the big man, like McGriff now, or McCovey and Mays, hitting when the ball's down, taking a full swing at it. He hits it on the end of the bat and it jumps off the bat real quick and it has been pitched in that area where you know if they hit it good it's gonna jump, then it gets out and dies. That is the toughest play to read off the bat. You make a step back and you continue watching the ball, you can adjust and catch some of them, but many will fall in front of you because you made one bad move. The other tough play is the line drive hit hard off the bat. Some of those will go down, some will go up, depending on where the ball hit on the bat. There is a certain hesitation so you can see if it's going to sink or what it's going to do.

Everybody accused me of playing a deep center. I played in Forbes Field against clubs with good power. Our club did not have good power, so naturally the other center fielders would play shallower than I did. But I didn't have any trouble coming in to get the ball. You play where your best coverage is. When Bob Skinner came up in left field, he had problems and I had to back him up quite a bit, but after awhile, he made all the plays. I didn't consider him a bad outfielder after he'd played out there. The young Willie Stargell was as talented a player as I've seen. Willie lost speed when he got bigger and matured. But Willie had good tools. He could throw with the best of them, his hands were good. If he would have stayed sleek, he could have played center field with the best of them. If I had to pick people who were sure to succeed, I'd pick Willie. Like the first time I saw Johnny Bench, and Mickey Mantle. I knew.

* * * * *

Back to Maz. We were roommates. We would get up, noon, one o'clock, we slept late. Play a night game, go out and eat after the game, you're not going to go to bed immediately, because you've eaten and anyway you're up to one or two o'clock in the morning. Both of us played every day, almost all the time, so we felt we needed the rest. We'd get up, eat breakfast. Get a paper. Read the paper. Go to the ballpark on the bus. We never went that early. In our minds, to get to the ballpark and sit around and not do anything, that was worse than getting there in time.

No, we didn't chew tobacco in the room. I've chewed ever since I started playing. If I'm out in the open or in the woods, I enjoy chewing. But not in a room. Maz was the same way. We didn't have too much to say but we got along well. I don't think we have ever had an argument as long as I've known him. I played with him for ten years, he coached for me for a year and I worked with him a little bit when I was managing Montreal. You don't have arguments with Maz. He's too good a guy. Anyway, I don't talk that much either. If I've got something to say I'll say it. There was hardly ever a night, rooming together, that we didn't go do things together. Unless, for some reason he had close friends or part of the family visiting.

Off-seasons, I went to Missouri and he stayed here. Maz's home is in the area around Pittsburgh. I never, ever stayed in the town I played in over the winter. I made that a policy. I always enjoyed Missouri, plus I felt if I stayed in town that my time would be the team's and not mine. I'm not one to say no. They don't like you to say no. I would have been going all the time. I think it turned out well. If you play this game, you play every day, start in February, no time off, you play weekends. If you don't play, you're associated with it in some way. You come to the ballpark, you might get rained out and so forth, but you're involved for eight months straight and it's time to get away. Getting away for four months a year kept me in it a lot longer. I think I would have had it up to here!

* * * * *

Maz was a leader who set an awfully good example for everybody on the field, because when he went to the plate, he was always bearing down, when he was out in the field he was always in the game, he never screwed up. He played to win, gave it his all. Baseball needs a lot more of that.

Maz worried about himself. He did everything in his power to do the job he was supposed to do. Perhaps naively, Maz thought everybody else would do that too. I agree with him. That's what you should do. Then you wouldn't have to have managers kicking somebody in the ass if he doesn't do his job.

Did I know I wanted to be a manager early on? The first four or five years I was just worried about staying in the game. But the second five years I started thinking about it. I've had a lot of people ask me, "Did you prepare to be a manager or coach while you were playing?" I said, no, I did not, I had enough problems taking care of the job I had to do.

I decided in 1965 that I wasn't going to play anymore. Physically I could have played three or four more years. I say that but you don't know. I couldn't keep my mind on the game and I had always prided myself on being alert, being in the game. I would catch myself in the outfield during a game in the 8th inning, close ballgame, I'd be thinking about something else. Things get away from you when that happens.

I made every mistake that you can make on the field; I just didn't make them too often. If I made one, I tried to let that be the last time. But I made them all.

Executing the cut-off properly is a big factor in the outfield. Ball off the wall or in the gap, if you don't play the relay right, the runners keep running. It's important to hit the first of two cut-off men; hitting his back-up, that's not as quick.

It was not human, from the distance he had to throw, for Maz to make good throws on double plays all the time, but he did it all the time. Now when you start making a hundred and forty-, a hundred and fifty-foot throws, from the fence to the relay man, it's a little bit tougher to be right on the money all the time. Maz used to get on me because throwing the ball in, I would short-hop him. Not when we were making relays, but when I was fielding a ground ball and throwing it back in. I was trying to keep from throwing it over his head, making sure he could handle it.

To grip the ball, you always try to come up with the seams up. You can't be worried about getting it just so, you haven't got time. You do learn, as you're coming out with it, to grab a seam. You might even spin the ball in your glove. Just something you get used to doing.

* * * * *

I didn't steal much. We'd hit and run a lot. I'd lead off, and next was Groat. There was never anybody better at handling the bat than Dick Groat. I didn't get thrown out at second, because if Groat swung and didn't get a hit he'd foul it somehow. Didn't always get me to second base, but he did most of the time.

That bad-hop ball I hit to Tony Kubek in the '60 Series? My first thought was, Oh shit! Seventh game, eighth inning, we're down three runs. Man on first, Bobby Shantz actually made a bad pitch. He got the ball up and I hit it good, but right at Kubek at short, for a sure double play. I ran hard, and about the time it got to him I saw it take a bad hop and hit him in the throat; that set up a five-run inning for us.

* * * * *

The toughest part of managing is handling people you've played with. People you've been pretty close to. They went out of their way to help me. Early in Clemente's career I thought he whined a little bit and I probably falsely accused him of not bearing down all the time, not playing sometime when he should, but look at the record, how many games he played, what he produced; that was not true, that was unfair. Roberto was new in our country and didn't know what to expect and what we expected of him, so it took him awhile to get his feet on the ground. I can't tell you how much I appreciate how he went about his business when he played for me.

Managing the 1972 Pirates, the year turned out exceptionally well. The only disappointment was we didn't win the playoffs. We had it and let it get away. The players were very disappointed. We were the best club in baseball, World Champions the year before, better in 1972 and we let it get away. It's one of those things that happen; that's why baseball is such a good game. There was nothing special during the game that really made the difference, it's just that we had fourteen chances to score runs and we didn't score them, but still led in the ninth inning when a couple of things happened.

The best thing about managing the Houston club was when I went there it was 43 games out of first; over a period of three or four years, we developed and ended up having a winner. Didn't win it all, we let it get away again in '80, had a lead in the 8th inning and lost it again. Like I say though, that's why it's a good game. But that was no fun. It wasn't as tough on me as it was on the players. Most would never have the opportunity again. They spend that much time on the club, have a chance to get into the World Series, get that close, right in the palm of their hand and it gets wiped out. I had been there before. I played there before, I coached there before, so I knew what we were missing. I told all the players I appreciated their efforts. It just didn't work out.

* * * * *

If I had to summarize Bill Mazeroski to someone who did not see him play, the impressive thing about him was that he did everything perfectly at second base. I backed him up for 10 years and never got a ball. You talk about instinctively doing something and continuing to do it when you know he's going to catch it, it's kind of hard, because the first time you don't do it, then he might miss one. I'm not exaggerating

"The toughest part of managing is handling people you've played with"

much. He may have booted one, but over ten years, not many. If he did, it probably didn't go on through him, he maybe bobbled it a little bit and maybe didn't quite get an out.

Another thing was Maz's ability to complete the double play from any position. That is a feat that nobody that I know of could do. Any kind of throw and he could complete the double play, if he had any kind of time at all. I think that's one of the greatest features of a second baseman. Bobby Richardson could turn a double play, could throw, same stumpy kind of guy, stayed right there. But he could not do it like Maz could do it, from all angles. Maz had no fear of anybody sliding into him or knocking him down. In fact, I've seen guys hit him and just slide down. He'd look down and say, "How ya doin'?"

I ran into Maz once, in the outfield in St. Louis. I didn't play the next inning and I was out for a game. It was like hitting a wall. I steered clear of Maz after that.

"Maz could make the routine plays. So could other second basemen. But only Maz could make the great plays."

– Bob Skinner

5

Bob Skinner

Bob Skinner joined the Pirates in 1954. After a year in the minors, he played left field for the Pirates from 1956 to 1963, when he was traded to the Reds. Traded again, to St. Louis the next year, Bob played on his second World Series champion in five years. Skinner played two more seasons in St. Louis, leading the National League with 15 pinch-hits in 1965. An All-Star in 1960, Bob hit .300 in '57, '58, and '62. His career batting average over twelve seasons is .277. One of the few men to hit a ball out of Forbes Field over the right field roof, Bob accomplished this feat twice. Skinner managed the Philadelphia Phillies in 1968 and 1969; by serving as hitting coach for the 1979 Pirates, he collected his third Series ring. Now retired from 42 years of playing and coaching baseball, Bob lives in La Jolla, California.

I was born in 1931 in La Jolla, just north of San Diego. We had a Triple A team in San Diego when I was growing up, the Padres of the Pacific Coast League. Of course then the most westerly major league city was St. Louis.

There was no television, and I wasn't interested in major league baseball so much as I was in the Padres. My friends and I used to try to sneak in to watch the Padres play; years later, I managed the team.

I went to college for one year in San Diego and went on to sign with the Pirates. I played in their minor league system for a year, then I was drafted into the Marine Corps. After spending two years in the Marine Corps, I got out in 1954. That's when I made the Pirates team.

Now Maz, I remember him coming out and trying out, I guess about 1955. Years later, after we were both out of baseball, Maz was telling me about the day he tried out. Maz said, "I had argyle socks on under my baseball socks. You told everyone, 'Look at this kid with the argyles!'"

When a kid like Maz works out, you see his baseball abilities immediately. Some guys with maybe more ability than Maz didn't make it. Bill had something else: a strong desire to be a winning player.

One thing about Maz – every day, he would arrive at the ballpark, put on his uniform, do his pre-game drill and work on his game. When something had to happen in a game for us to win, Maz was usually involved. It got to the point where late in the game I was hoping that, some way or another, Maz could get his hands on the ball. Because if he did, an out was automatic, especially in tight situations.

Maz was a private guy, very quiet, but he played great ball.

I had an excellent ringside seat out there in left. I could see all the plays in the infield. Maz could make the routine plays. So could other second basemen. But only Maz could make the great plays.

Bill was a powerful hitter, too. Of course he hit the home runs in the 1960 World Series to win Game 1 and Game 7, but he had a lot of key hits. He would drive in runs year after year to help win games. Bill was a winning ballplayer who would shine in tough situations.

Baserunners found him very hard to take out in the middle of the infield. He had guys bouncing off him all the time, trying to break up double plays. They would bear down with one thing in mind, break up that double play. But Maz had those great big legs. He never seemed to get hurt. He had bruises but never seemed to have many major injuries, which was amazing. Maz stayed right up on second base and made the play, regardless of who was coming. I have never seen anybody quicker at getting rid of the ball.

Bobby Richardson of the Yankees was the closest. I only saw Richardson in the World Series. But Maz's ball took a right angle turn to first. He just barely reached for it. Maz had to have good hands. I don't think he even caught the ball on a double play. He just had it at the top of his glove, a small kind of glove. The ball just hit at the top. It was so fast. I never saw him reach for the ball in the pocket. You see a lot of players do that, especially with the bigger gloves.

* * * * *

It seemed that Maz was out there every day, played every game, every inning, never complained about anything. Remember Stan Williams, the Dodgers' pitcher? Williams was a hard fastball pitcher and he would throw at Maz, behind his head even. Maz never showed any emotion; he just kept on hitting.

He would just mind his own business and play his game. He showed leadership by doing that. Our manager, Danny Murtaugh, loved him. In fact, Murtaugh used to use some of us he liked for scapegoats. Every time he had a meeting to chew the players out he would point out Mazeroski, Skinner, and Stuart, because he knew that we could take the criticism. It went off us like water off a duck's back. To fire the team up, Danny had to get on somebody, so he'd jump on us, which was fine.

Twice I hit a ball over the right field roof at Forbes Field. When you hit one that hard you know it's a home run, in that second. It has to be hit high and long to get out, because the right field roof was 86 feet from the ground.

I played first base as a rookie, and I wasn't the best in left field when I started out there. Bill Virdon was a big help to me because he was catching everything from his position in center field. I worked very hard on my defense, daily, and that paid off. Virdon, Clemente, and Murtaugh helped me, but there was nothing more beneficial than playing every day. I could always hit. But when I was a first baseman in the minor leagues there was only about a fifty-fifty chance that I was going to catch the ball!

Clemente, of course, would throw runners out at home. So would Bill Virdon. Very seldom did I do that.

"I worked very hard on my defense, daily, and that paid off"

We never gave the other team too much room with an extra base. Our team knew how to play the game and that's why we won. You see a lot of mistakes now, like failing to bunt runners over. We took pride in bunting. Things have changed; now offensive stats are everything.

In Game 7 of the 1960 World Series, I was called upon to sacrifice bunt. So I did. I could sacrifice any time I wanted to. I was that confident.

I could steal a base, too. I led the Pirates three years in stolen bases; I don't remember how many.

I played in the Dodgers' last game in Ebbets Field, and in the Giants' last game in the Polo Grounds. It just so happened our team was there that year. With the Cardinals, I hit the last home run in the old Busch Stadium, into a little garden in right center field.

When you played left field at Forbes Field in my day, they had blue laws. They couldn't sell any beer in the ballpark on Sundays. Every Sunday we had a double-header. Families would come from all over and bring coolers in. They would drink everything in those coolers and throw dry ice at me. It would smoke in the grass. It was really entertaining.

I loved Forbes Field, of course, because I was a straightaway type of hitter. I hit to the gaps.

The scoreboard was out there in left field. Say I had a line drive coming my way. The guy who ran the scoreboard could tell from his vantage point inside if the ball was going to be over my head. I would be going back and he would yell at me to play it off the wall! Something else – if you caught the last out, I never did this, but some guys did – you could leave the field by heading right into the scoreboard.

* * * * *

I was just a grinder. I worked every day. I started out one year, 1961, hitting .098 or something about thirty days into the season. Then on a Saturday I got five straight hits. That was a highlight. I went home and opened up a bottle. Invited all the neighbors! Five hits in a row doesn't happen too often to anybody.

Getting traded from Pittsburgh to Cincinnati in 1963 was an emotional thing. I loved the Pirates. I didn't want to be traded. But the previous year, even though I'd hit .300, I'd run into the fence in Milwaukee and hurt my back. Willie Stargell was ready to replace me, so the Pirates wanted me to move on.

After a short time with the Reds, I reunited in St. Louis with Dick Groat. In 1964 our team beat the Yankees, who haven't lost very many World Series. Dick and I are two guys who have beaten them twice.

* * * * *

The fans around the league could identify with Maz because he was a workingman's ballplayer. Fans appreciated the way he played hard every day. Maz never complained. He was like a millworker.

Maz had great instinct and intelligence on the ball field; he always did the right thing. That's because Maz was a natural ballplayer who worked hard.

"I had a ringside seat out in left field watching Maz play second base...you just kept shaking your head, saying, 'Damn!'"

– Willie Stargell

6

Willie Stargell

Hall-of-Famer Willie Stargell hit 475 home runs in 21 years with the Pittsburgh Pirates. The only man to hit a ball out of Dodger Stadium (he did it twice), Willie hit 7 of the 18 balls to clear Forbes Field's roof in right field. A seven-time All-Star, Willie hit .300 three times, 30 or more home runs six times, and 3 home runs in a game on four occasions. In 1979, as a 39-year-old converted left fielder, "Pops" led National League first basemen with a .997 fielding percentage. That year the Pirates' captain was co-M.V.P. of the league, and M.V.P. of both the league playoffs and the World Series, won with the help of Willie's decisive home run in the seventh game. A .282 lifetime hitter, Willie's strikeout total of 1,936 is a distant second to Reggie Jackson's 2,597 whiffs. An intimidating slugger and inspirational leader, Willie now works with the Atlanta Braves' farm system.

Funny thing about Maz. The team would go to different cities and you would always see that second baseman moseying over towards Maz, familiarizing himself with his style of play. Nobody could turn a double play like Maz.

His feet were always dancing. I noticed that, playing left field. It would amaze me how Maz could be in one position, with the ball off to his left or right, and you would think he'd have to be a speed demon to get in front of it, but he was always there. His range was much greater than his speed.

Maz not only made good catches, he made good throws to the first baseman. People don't realize how strong Maz was. I've seen big guys go into him at second base, guys like Ron Stone, and he'd just tear them up. Maz was a very gifted second baseman. I truly would tell anybody, Maz should be in the Hall of Fame. Maz may not have hit 400 home runs or driven in 2000 runs, but look how many runs he saved. Fielding his position, he was perfection. When you talk about second basemen, those who know anything about the game are going to say Mazeroski, without a breath of air.

Baseball was all I ever did. I remember the anxiety of wanting to hit and throw something every day. I lived with my aunt in Florida for six years, before 1951. I was not even ten years old. I had chores that I'd neglect because my aunt would come home at 3:15 from her job and leave early in the morning in the summertime. As soon as she was out I was gone playing ball. It wasn't organized, but I was out playing. Every day, at a quarter to three, I'd be running home trying to do those chores in less than a half an hour. They never got done. I got whups on my butt to prove it. I had more love for baseball than I did for my butt.

Growing up in California we lived in a housing project. Policemen would come through the projects and have tryouts for guys they were trying to keep off the streets. I heard about this police league, tried out, and made the team. I was nothing but a rail. I remember the uniform I got, boy, did I look like Louie the sack man! But I was so proud of that thing. If I could have run 30 miles per hour I would have gone up like a hot air balloon. That's how much room I had in that uniform. I treated it like a fine Italian suit. It was itchy tweed, but that didn't matter.

My first glove was a right-handed glove, so I had to use it the wrong way. The part that went across the wrist had a button. That made it snazzy because I could take it off, unbutton the button, put the glove on my belt loop and not lose it. Finally a guy sold me, for three dollars and fifty cents, a left-handed glove. That was the cat's meow. That was my girlfriend. We slept together. I didn't want to risk losing it. Kept it clean, didn't let anyone use it.

Next to the projects was a railroad yard. We'd sneak in and hit rocks with two-by-fours over boxcars. After a while the vision came: I was hitting home runs in a stadium. People were cheering. It was really vivid, a recurring vision I can still remember. People would ask me: "What do you want to do when you grow up?" Back then I never hesitated to tell them. I would be a professional ballplayer. People would laugh and discourage me, tell me no way could I come out of the projects.

Curt Motton lived in Estuary Housing Projects. Tommy Harper lived in Webster Projects. We went to high school together and on to junior college. We signed at the same time and are all still in the game: Curt's with Baltimore, Tommy's with Montreal, and I'm with the Braves.

I just had a burning desire to play the game of baseball. You become a student and you never stop learning. I went to the minor leagues, following my dream. I didn't care where it took me. I didn't want to be an ordinary ballplayer in the big leagues. In getting there, I paid too huge a price to just be ordinary. So much inside of me needed to be expressed: I wanted to be better at throwing, at hitting, at thinking on the field and being alert. I didn't mind screwing up. I wanted to be totally aggressive as a player called upon to score and drive in important runs.

I encountered racism in the minors. But I didn't have any hatred. There's an old saying, "He who angers you has conquered you." I would get mad and disappointed. But I wanted to play baseball and do my job so well that the next person coming behind me would have difficulty duplicating it. I was going to be a Monday through Sunday ballplayer.

*　*　*　*　*　*

I thoroughly enjoyed every minute at Forbes Field, being close to the fans. I was so close that I practically knew the folks who sat in the bleachers. The scoreboard was out in left field. You could actually go in it. If I caught the last out of the inning, there was a guy in the scoreboard with a big popcorn and something cold for me to drink.

I had met Maz at spring training and marvelled at him. Of course I knew him before he knew me, because of the 1960 World Series. I knew about him and Clemente, all these guys I had seen on television.

I remember making the big leagues, getting the word in Columbus, Bob Veale and me. Bob had an old Studebaker that we drove to Pittsburgh. That three-hour drive seemed to take two days with all the anticipation, excitement. I think we got there on a Wednesday. Thursday was an off day, which made things worse. Friday, going into that clubhouse at Forbes Field, at first I didn't know how to get in. Then I got on the field, stood at the top of the dugout steps and looked around. So much history there. They had a plaque on the right field wall; when Babe Ruth played his last game in Forbes Field, he hit three home runs, and the last one was over the right field roof, 86 feet up.

I walked around in a daze. We were playing the Giants that weekend. Danny Murtaugh told me to get a bat and pinch-hit. Stu Miller was pitching. As I went to the bat rack, our first baseman, Dick Stuart, said, "Hey rook – when you strike out, don't feel bad." What a terrible thing to say! I did strike out. Stu Miller threw me a change-up and I swung at it and swung again before it got to the plate. You never forget the first at-bat.

The Pirate veterans wanted to see if I was going to be a come-and-go-quickly ballplayer. I had to keep getting better, keep working hard. Clemente and Bill Virdon helped me learn how to play left field. I'd see Virdon getting his work in religiously, every day. Clemente worked with me a great deal on technique, to make sure I knew what I was doing when a ball was hit, what position I would have to get myself in, to throw properly and accurately. I soon learned to play left field, and I wanted the ball to be hit to me in tough situations.

Clemente also helped challenge me as a hitter to drive in runs, to want to be the guy to come up with the big hit, or if I didn't get a big hit, to leave such an impression that the opposition would take a deep breath.

My philosophy of hitting was simple: hit the ball hard somewhere. Hard ground balls. Hard line drives. I'd analyze the pitcher and see if he was a strike-out pitcher – if so I didn't want to go deep in the count. If he was not overpowering I didn't mind being patient, because I'd get a chance to see all his pitches, with less chance of being fooled.

In 1966 I had nine hits in a row. I was just in a groove: the baseball looked like a basketball. Then again, it looks like a B.B. when you're not hitting well. I hit for the cycle once in St. Louis; the starting pitcher was Ray Washburn and I hit everything that was pitched. I remember the home run going completely out of Sportsman's Park. Double to right center field, triple to left center, single up the middle.

This gag photo addresses what every National League pitcher knew: when Willie Stargell was swinging a hot bat, no hitter was more feared

With long home runs, hitting the ball out of Dodger Stadium, or out of Forbes Field, there really is a different feel. It's almost like the bat bends when you nail one. You see the ball going and going and it's just unbelievable.

Some pitchers, I don't care what I did, I couldn't come close to them. Joe Hoerner of the Cardinals. They'd bring him in just for me. My teammates would laugh: "Come on back Willie, we're going to send the Girl Scouts up there, let the bat boy hit."

Speaking of left-handers, I was on a U.S.O. tour of Vietnam when we met up with these rock apes on Hontra Island, the radar base. We were riding in a jeep with a cage around it. Most of the rocks the rock apes were throwing were just tick, tick, ticking and all of a sudden you would hear some go pow! pow! I was looking around and there was this left-handed monkey. I remember saying, "I'd hate to hit against him!"

That tour was devastating, more than I thought it would be. We met a lot of guys that weren't going to make it. One guy was a triple amputee, both legs cut off, with one arm. He was just as happy as he could be to see us. He told us to tell his parents that he was all right, he was coming home. I went over there with Mudcat Grant, Merv Rettenmund, Bob Prince and Eddie Watt – we all felt good because those servicemen were glad to see us.

* * * * *

Back to Maz. You'd see balls hit and you'd think, that's a base hit but no, Maz got to it and you'd think, damn, how did Maz get to that ball? Maz made tough double plays look so easy. I had a ringside seat out in left field watching Maz play second base...you just kept shaking your head, saying, "Damn!" The stuff he used to do at second base, nobody else could do. Like Brooks Robinson at third...Maz is one of those exceptional individuals.

So many great plays. One day you would see one and say, Oh, I've never seen one like that! Next day, same thing. Maz would get a throw that second basemen today come off the bag for, scoop the damn thing up on one hop and throw it back to the first baseman and again, I've never seen anything like that! Then a couple of days later, Maz gets off a throw in mid-air with a runner right on him and you forget about the day before. Maz was always topping himself.

Joe Morgan and I grew up together and are good friends. As good as Joe was, if somebody says, "Who is the greatest second baseman?", and Joe is standing right there, I say, "Mazeroski." Joe doesn't take any offense.

Maz was a good RBI man too. He was the kind of guy you wanted up there in key situations.

* * * * *

In 1971, if I hadn't messed up my knee in the Astrodome in August, I could have put giant numbers on the board, but I twisted my left knee in the outfield. Every day that knee would swell and cause agony. I had torn cartilage in the knee, which as a left-handed hitter I needed to push off from, to thrust into the ball.

Dr. Ferguson, the team doctor, asked me to have an operation. I didn't want to stop; I wanted to be in the Series. So I struggled that last part of the season and I'd even get it from the players, but I didn't care, because we were winning. Then the media got on me for not producing. I didn't offer any excuses.

The day after the World Series I was in the hospital getting the knee cut on. Now in my left knee it's bone on bone. I've learned to live with it and wouldn't have done anything different. Unless there is a bone showing or you have a broken back, you are supposed to be out there.

Home runs I remember? In 1972, Jarry Park, Montreal, I hit one over the right field scoreboard into the municipal swimming pool off of Dan McGinn, a left-handed pitcher for the Expos. The prior series in Pittsburgh I'd been anticipating a slider and Dan threw me a tailing fastball. Blood was spurting everywhere; Dan and some of the Expos were laughing. So we went to Montreal and here comes the fastball, which I was waiting for. Into the pool was my way of paying them back.

In the seventh game of the 1979 World Series, I hit one off Scott McGregor of the Orioles. It just made it over the fence. At the 1965 All-Star game, against Mudcat Grant, I hit the ball where they had a band, out in the right center field bullpen, and the ball landed inside a tuba. I hear it made a funny sound.

I'm still in the game as a special assistant to the Atlanta Braves' G.M., taking a look at talent. With a young hitter I look for bat speed. If you don't have it, you can't buy it. Hank Aaron had unbelievable bat speed with less effort and with the best results of anybody I've ever seen. Mays, Clemente, Frank Robinson all had exceptional bat speed. Now when I'm looking at middle infielders, I look for quick feet. Like Maz had.

Bill Mazeroski was a player you wanted on your ball club. He was a thinking man's player. Knew what he was doing at all times. Not fancy. Steady. You could count on him. As a person, Maz is just a dream. The moment you meet him he makes you feel comfortable. He always has a smile, a pleasant greeting for you.

Our pitcher would look out there at second base, take a deep breath and sigh, "I've got the best out there." In any double play situation he'd turn the ball over and get it hit on the ground in Bill's direction. Then you'd start walking off the field.

That's Bill Mazeroski, number 9. Very dependable. I'm glad to know him.

"He was one of a kind out there. Maz did so many things that never showed up in the box score."

– Bob Friend

7

Bob Friend

Bob Friend pitched for the Pirates from 1951-1965; over a stretch of twelve seasons, Bob never missed a start. He made 497 career starts, winding up with 427 decisions, a record of 197-230. The only pitcher in major league history to lead a league in E.R.A. with a last-place team (2.83 in 1955), Bob had minimal support from Pirate teams that played .400 ball in the '50s. The indefatigable Friend led the National League in innings pitched in 1956 (314) and 1957 (277); he would rack up 3,611 innings in his distinguished career. Friend led the National League with 22 wins in 1958, and with 5 shutouts in 1962; he hurled 36 shutouts all told. An All-Star with the Pirates in 1956, 1958 and 1960, Bob concluded his career with the Yankees and Mets in 1966. Bob Friend used his prodigious memory to catalogue strengths and weaknesses of every hitter he faced; today he applies it to the insurance business in Pittsburgh, where he works just a stone's throw from Three Rivers Stadium.

I was born in West Lafayette, Indiana, November 24th, 1930. By the time I was five I belonged to an athletic club. It was mainly geared to football, but we did play all sports. I developed a strong arm, and was able to throw the ball harder than most kids my age. Scouts starting looking at me when I was thirteen. That's when I decided I wanted to go into baseball.

I was going to sign with Stan Feezle of the Brooklyn Dodgers, who had signed Carl Erskine and Gil Hodges, both Indiana boys. But Branch Rickey left Brooklyn and took his scouting staff with him to Pittsburgh. Stan was a great salesman and scout, and I thought it was a great opportunity to sign with the Pirates in 1950 for an $18,000 bonus. Pretty good money then.

I was 19, going to Purdue to play football, but I opted for baseball and was sent to Waco, Texas, Class B. It was a good hitting league. Most of those players were in their thirties. I learned how to pitch down there.

One day I was told I was going to go up to Indianapolis; I pitched a no-hitter against Wichita Falls that night, quite a thrill.

The next year I had a good spring with the Pirates and was called up to the main club in 1951, and stayed there because Branch Rickey was rebuilding with young players.

The Pirates had poor ball clubs in the first five years of my career. It was a learning process for the entire club.

And then some good things started to happen. That's when I first met Maz. He came up at 19 in 1956 from the Hollywood team. We had heard about this fancy fielder out there, see. Believe me, Maz was outstanding from the start.

He had a great attitude and didn't say much, just did his job every day. He had this knack. Maz is a great athlete, and he had those great feet, he could get rid of the ball. He was a good, timely hitter too. We had gone through a lot of second basemen and it was a real treat to have somebody behind you like that. I mean it.

* * * * *

Why was my arm strong? I used to work in the feed mill and then pitch a ballgame that night. I did this for three or four summers. Builds up strength in your arm. I never had arm trouble. I was able to pitch every third or fourth day. Like Bob Feller, my hero when I was a kid.

Nobody smoked in my family, but if I sent in so many Old Gold wrappers, I got a baseball bible. I used to do that every year. I'd find out who smoked Old Gold cigarettes. This is the way we'd operate. Baseball was it.

My dad encouraged me. He didn't get to see me play pro baseball because he passed away when I was about to be a sophomore in high school. He is why I went back to Purdue and got my degree.

I pitched close to four thousand innings and never had a sore arm. I threw the ball every day. Sometimes I pitched twenty minutes of batting practice in between starts. I'd lob the ball in the outfield. Didn't do any throwing in the winter-time.

It wasn't until Maz got in there at second base, with Billy Virdon in center field and Groat at shortstop that we had guys who could catch the ball and take you out of the big inning. That's what Maz was able to do for the pitchers. Maz would make some great plays and he could turn a double play. Unless you're going to strike out eighteen batters a game, you need players like that to survive.

I was around the plate a lot; I didn't like to stretch the counts out. If my sinker ball was working, I'd try to get batters to hit it.

The base on balls made a lot of managers go to their grave early; we got that drilled into us from the start. Get ahead of the hitters. Don't lose them. If you pitch behind the hitters all the time, you're not going to have good fielding behind you. The fielders are going to be on their heels.

My first manager with the Pirates was Billy Meyer, who came over from the Yankees in '48. He was a good pitcher's manager. Billy liked me early on because I threw the ball hard and I challenged the hitters; he'd say, "That's the old Yankees style. I like it."

Then came Fred Haney, a good manager, and Bobby Bragan.

I liked Bobby. He pitched me on two days' rest, five or six times one year. When you were hot, he'd work you.

Danny Murtaugh was just a great manager, and a wonderful man. Harry Walker was maybe not as good at handling pitchers as other managers, but he was certainly dedicated to the game. Clyde King was his pitching coach, so I was pretty lucky.

Did I ever tell the manager in late innings that I wanted to stay in the game? There was some negotiation at times; but remember, we had ElRoy Face. He came on strong in '56 and was effective for many years. You aren't going to argue too much about Face coming in to relieve you. With men on base, he could strike batters out with that forkball. But sure, you want to stay in the game. And we did pitch more complete games then because that's the way the game was. Today, they get five innings out of you, that's a quality start. Makes you shake your head. The game has changed.

I pitched with Vernon Law, Harvey Haddix, ElRoy, all very good arms; pitched against Robin Roberts, Warren Spahn, Lew Burdette, Larry Jansen, Sal Maglie, Don Newcombe, Carl Erskine. Every one was a tough competitor.

* * * * *

There are still great players in today's game, but pitching has been diluted with twenty-eight teams. I don't think the staffs are as strong, throughout the staff, as they were back in the '50s, with twelve fewer teams to supply pitchers for.

Prospects' arms don't seem to be as strong as they used to be. Maybe they baby their arms. There are other things to do now. All we did was play baseball. None of that computer game stuff.

Haddix's 12-inning perfect game in 1959? I was rooming with Harvey on that road trip. It was amazing. It wasn't any fluke. Nobody got close to hitting him through twelve innings. It's a shame he lost the game in the 13th. His breaking stuff was outstanding, he was extra fast that night, and he had complete command of his location. You could just see it in his eyes. Harvey was in that zone.

In 1960, I pitched better than any time in my life. Four shutouts. Strikeouts, 183. Base on balls, 45. It could have been a 25-win year, but it wasn't. I went into the thirteenth inning a couple of times with no decisions. I was out of only two or three games all year. And I pitched a hell of a lot better in '60 than I did in '58, when I won 22 games. Because every time I walked out there in '58, I had three or four runs by the third inning.

Our 1960 team didn't make mistakes. Timely hitting. Good bench. Good starting pitching and relief. You weren't safe with our club going into the seventh inning if you had a lead on us.

Cincinnati had a 5-0 lead against us in April. It's getting dark, the second game of a double-header. Soon the score's 5-3, two men on, two out – Skinner hits the ball in the second deck. The Reds' manager, Hutchinson, was so damned mad he charged through the runway knocking lightbulbs out with his fist! That was one game we pulled out.

Another was against Koufax in Los Angeles. He had a 3-0 lead with two outs in the ninth. We won 4-3. We came from behind to win 20 to 30 times from the seventh inning on that year.

Same thing with beating the Yankees in the 1960 World Series – we never gave up. There were ten of us who played on those bad teams in the '50s – to win a championship after that was tremendous. It was the first time in thirty-three years anybody had won anything in the city of Pittsburgh. We were the toast of the town.

Pitching into the 1960's, I was trying to adjust to losing a little bit on the fastball and the breaking ball by trying to pick up a different type of a slider. I was sold to the Yankees.

I wasn't able to pick up another effective pitch. A lot of guys come up with a knuckle ball or a spitter. Warren Spahn picked up a screwball when he was thirty-two years old. He had lost the steam on his fastball. Spahn won twenty games nine times in the next eleven years, from age 32 to 42. Threw a couple of no-hitters, too.

I still had a good arm, but I retired and went into a little investment business. I was controller for eight years in Allegheny County.

* * * * *

Highlights for me in baseball were starting and winning two All-Star games. My first All-Star game in '56, Griffith Stadium, I won that. Facing guys like Berra, Mantle, Kell, Ted Williams, I pitched three scoreless innings and struck out Williams with the bases loaded in my last inning. Glad to get out of there alive! I ended up winning that game and one in Kansas City in 1960. The twenty-two games won in 1958, and several one-hitters. Staying in one town so darn long was great, too. Fifteen years with Pittsburgh. I was very fortunate.

The first game I played in Pittsburgh was special, too – we were thrilled to death to even be here. You're 20 and you're in the major leagues, brother. Back when guys were spending

"For twelve years, I didn't miss a start"

seven, eight years in the minor leagues, here I'm fortunate to be up in one year. Most people thought Pittsburgh was smoky back then; I thought Pittsburgh was beautiful.

The first time I saw Maz? Boy, was he thin. We kid each other now about being too heavy. You could see he was a great athlete. A lot of agility. Everything seemed to flow, the hands, everything. And he loved the game.

I was impressed with Maz over the years because he never complained, and gave you a consistent game every time. Maz made big plays that you just took for granted. Played every day. Durable. Tough to take out on a double play. Nobody took him out. Other second basemen worried about getting hit, but not Maz. At the plate he got a lot of timely hits. He was dangerous in late innings.

Maz did have occasional power – he hit 138 home runs. But the thing about Maz, he'd keep you in a ballgame with those great plays. Keep you out of the big inning. Just a good guy to have on the club.

Sometimes leaders become leaders by their performance, and that's the way Maz was. He didn't miss much. Maz was quiet but he knew what was going on. Maz was pretty perceptive about people and the game.

Maz made so many great double plays that I can't tell you about a specific one. A big play happened every game. Maz did it every day.

We'd marvel at him, but after a while, even though Maz was so good, we'd take him for granted. Like he was part of the ground crew. Eddie Dunn was the head of the ground crew. There's Maz. There's Eddie.

* * * * *

The most unusual thing I saw in my career? Hard to say, but when the Pirates were not a good team in the early '50s, and Ralph Kiner would make the last out in the bottom of the seventh, a lot of times fans would just leave Forbes Field, figuring Kiner had had his last at-bat! On the other hand, I pitched Opening Day in 1952 in Pittsburgh against Ewell Blackwell; I threw a 2-hit shutout in a snowstorm – and those were big snowflakes – before 33,000 fans packing Forbes Field!

I can remember when Ralph Kiner hit his two hundred and fiftieth home run in Boston. We celebrated his home run with champagne at the Copley Plaza. I'll never forget that. Kiner picked up the whole tab. That was first class.

In a baseball encyclopedia, my nickname is "Warrior," but I really don't know how they got that. I did play football in high school. I was a pretty good tailback.

Maybe somebody called me an old warrior because for twelve years, I didn't miss a start. If you're not keeping your team in the game, you're not going to be called on to pitch. Most of the time when I pitched, we had a chance to win the game. There were a lot of pitchers who just didn't have the arm to sustain a full season.

Maz was the complete player: durability and perseverance, athleticism, dedication to his job. What more can you say? He was the best second baseman I ever saw. Never hurt, consistent, a great attitude.

He was one of a kind out there. Maz did so many things that never showed up in the box score. Intangibles. Maz should be proud of his defensive abilities – any team that doesn't have defense doesn't win. I don't care who you are. You don't win.

"Maz would constantly come up with balls we thought were base hits. You're running over to back up a base and here Maz has got the ball and he's throwing that hitter out!"

– Vernon Law

8

Vernon Law

Vernon Law spent his entire 16-year career with Pittsburgh, from 1950-51, and 1954-67. An All-Star in 1960, Law won the Cy Young Award that year with a record of 20-9, including a league-leading 18 complete games. Vernon won one All-Star game and saved another that season; he won Game 1 and Game 4 in the Pirates' 1960 Series triumph. The last major leaguer to pitch 18 innings in a game, Vernon's career totals were 162 wins and 147 losses, with a 3.77 E.R.A. Law was National League Comeback Player of the Year in 1965. A high priest in the Mormon church, Vernon spends time keeping track of his large family and helping with Utah youth programs.

I was born in 1930 in Meridian, Idaho. In grade school, my older brother, Evan, and I did everything together, hunted, fished, played football, basketball, baseball. We started out early with hard ball, about fifth grade in a little teeny country school outside of Meridian. This was just before the war, in 1941. We moved down to California, where my Dad worked at a submarine base. In California we got to play in quite a few baseball games.

Back in Meridian, after the war was over, we played American Legion ball. My junior year of high school, our little town didn't have enough players to field a team, so three of us went to Boise to play on their team. It was one of the twelve best teams in the United States. We won the district, the state, the regional and went to the sectional tournament in Billings, Montana. That's where I met Babe Ruth and got an autographed ball from the Babe. That stimulated my interest!

As soon as I graduated from high school, I signed a professional contract. It was kind of interesting how I signed with the Pirates. Senator Welker of Idaho saw my brother and me playing in a tournament in Idaho. He was an attorney then, not a senator yet. There was a real good ballgame going, score was 0-0 going into the last inning.

They put up a midget to hit against me. This kid looked like he was 3 1/2 feet tall. I know if the ball had gotten away from me and hit him, it would have killed him. I threw three straight strikes and struck him out. This impressed Mr. Welker and he called Bing Crosby. He had gone to college with Bing, who was Vice President of the Pirates back then, in 1948.

Bing called the front office, Babe Herman came out to scout me, and by the time I graduate, I've got nine organizations wanting to sign me. With that situation today, you could sign for a million dollars or better. Back then I got the pen I signed with.

The reason I signed with the Pirates was all the other scouts that came in didn't leave too good of an impression with my parents. They would come in smoking cigars. My Dad allowed no smoking in the house; he'd say, "You can come in but that cigar's got to stay outside." Babe Herman and Herman Welker were the last ones to come in. They brought a box of chocolates and a bouquet of flowers for my mother; halfway through the conversation the phone rings. On the other end of the line is Bing Crosby! My mother just about fainted on the spot.

Pittsburgh needed pitchers. The chances of getting to the big leagues in a hurry were good. My first two years there, we had a terrible, terrible ball club, as you can see from our record. I felt if I didn't pitch a shutout and hit a home run, my chances of winning were not good.

It wasn't until I'd been in the big leagues awhile and the Dodgers had moved to L.A. that Bing Crosby happened to be in the clubhouse when I was pitching and said, "I want to tell you something about your signing that you probably don't know. Babe Herman and Herman Welker bought a big box of cigars and passed them out to all the other scouts who didn't know about the Mormons, that they didn't smoke or drink!"

My Dad was very, very strict. When he told you to do something, you had better do it or you got the leather belt. We worked hard as kids on the farm. Back then it was horse and plow. We couldn't afford a tractor. It was tough work. Yet my Dad was quite an amateur ballplayer himself. One day he pitched a double-header and won both games. I'm sure I got some of those genes.

* * * * *

I started in the minors in Santa Rosa, California, Class D. The next season I spent a full year in Davenport, Iowa, B ball. Bill Burwell, my manager, taught me a little bit more about pitching. Then New Orleans, playing in the Southern Association for the Pelicans. Joe Brown was the general manager. I spent two months there before I was called up in 1950. I spent the '50 and '51 seasons with the Pirates, then was in the Army for two years.

I played on the post team and some sandlot. I was at Ft. Eustis, Virginia, and played for a good little town team there in Seaford.

My first two big league starts were unusual. The first game, I had a 4-2 lead against Robin Roberts, men on second and third, two outs, and a little fly ball goes over the infield. Stan Rojek goes back and hollers, "I've got it, I've got it"; Ralph Kiner comes in, Stan hears Ralph's feet and Ralph can hear Stan coming, they both stop and the ball falls in. Either one could have had it; both runs score. Now we go to Philadelphia for my second game, again facing Robin Roberts, the same situation comes up and again, they both stop, the ball falls in, both runs score and I'm out of there. I lost both games.

I remember my first impression of Maz: here's a kid who doesn't say two words. So shy. I didn't know if he was ever going to come out of his shell. He would go about his work very quietly. You couldn't help but like him, he was a great kid. I really liked his play in the infield; it had been some time since we'd had a good second baseman you could rely on.

Bobby Bragan was our manager then. Every time Maz would come up in a tough situation, he would be looking over his shoulder because he knew he was going to be taken out for a pinch hitter. So he never developed confidence in his hitting until Murtaugh took over. I remember Danny saying "Maz, you're my man," right on the bench. "Look, you're going to get the job done. You're a hitter." Maz started to improve and became one of our better clutch hitters later on. I give Murtaugh credit for developing Maz's self-confidence. Danny wanted Maz to take charge and he did.

When we got to the World Series in 1960, everybody was rooting for everybody and there was no professional jealousy. It wasn't always that way. In the early '50s, if the team was playing one night, and you were going to pitch the next night, you were hoping we didn't win tonight. Because we never won two in a row. You'd think, maybe they'll score some runs for me tomorrow night if they don't tonight.

In 1955 I pitched 18 innings in a game I wasn't even supposed to pitch. I had only had two days' rest. Our starting pitcher came in sick, I'm in the outfield getting my exercise, preparing for my next start in a couple of days and Murtaugh hollers, "Hey Deacon, can you pitch?" I go in and change shirts, sit down and get ready for the ballgame.

Both teams scored early. The score was tied in the ninth inning, 2-2. We were playing the Braves. We came up to bat and Murtaugh let me stay in. Well, we get to the twelfth inning and I'm still getting them out, so he let me stay in. Fifteenth inning now, it's my turn to hit and he said, "I'd better take you out," and I said, "I've been pitching this long, let me win or lose it." Murtaugh felt sorry for me and let me stay in. Eighteenth inning, my turn to bat, he said, "I've got to take you out, Deacon. If you injure your arm or hurt yourself, they'll run me out of town!"

Bob Friend relieved me and gave up a run in the nineteenth. We came back to score two runs in our half of the nineteenth. Friend got credit for the victory. No justice in this game, I guess.

Over eighteen innings I gave up nine hits, struck out twelve, walked three, and gave up two runs, in a game I wasn't supposed to pitch – on two days' rest. I came back four days later against Cincinnati and pitched thirteen innings before I won that one. That's unheard of today. They don't let a pitcher pitch over six innings anymore. That's a "quality start." We were expected to finish what we started.

In another game from that era I was ahead of the Giants, 11-1. Ninth inning, I get the first man out, then maybe I walk a man, a base hit, a couple of guys get on base, a couple of runs score, another guy gets a base hit, run scores, Murtaugh takes me out. Four pitchers later, ElRoy Face comes in. The Giants get a couple of hits off of him too and score some more. So now the score is 11-10, bases are loaded, 3-2 count on the hitter! ElRoy makes the batter pop it up back over the infield where we've got three guys: our shortstop, an outfielder, and Maz. At the last minute, Maz dives at the ball, catching it about a foot off the ground for the last out. One of the more bizarre games I was ever in! It taught me that no lead is ever safe.

In 1959, when ElRoy lost only once and won eighteen, seven of those were my victories. That's a lot of poaching! I tried the best I could to finish what I started. I hated coming out of the ballgame and leaving it for someone else.

That season, Harvey Haddix's 12-inning perfect game was

unbelievable. No really tough chances. It was a fun game to sit and watch. Harvey wasn't giving up any hits and he was hitting the corners. Old Harv wore them down, it just didn't work out for him and he lost the game in the thirteenth.

*   *   *   *   *

I was a control pitcher. Hit the spots, pitch to hitters' weaknesses. Don't walk guys and get yourself in trouble. One year I walked 40 in 270 innings. You walk one guy, you should strike out two. Hold the other team to three runs or less, you've got a good chance to win. Be as stingy as you can giving up runs.

I tried to be a complete ball player: a good fielder and a good bunter who could get runners over. I kept myself in a lot of ballgames.

I wanted to pitch all of the time. All of us did. During my whole career Friend was perhaps considered the ace of the staff. He started every year pitching the first ballgame. That didn't bother me.

Winning the Cy Young Award in 1960 wasn't such a big deal. Two or three other guys could have won it. Warren Spahn, Ernie Broglio. I never looked at myself as the best pitcher in the league. That year we won the World Series and I pitched in two All-Star games.

What an honor to play on an All-Star team. I saved the first game in Kansas City. Two or three days later we played in New York; I pitched three innings and got the victory.

We won games in 1960 that we had no business winning. Going into the ninth inning down three runs, with two outs, somebody would get a walk, then a base hit, walk, home run, we end up winning the game. That happened 20 or 30 times, where we won the game in the last three innings.

"Vinegar Bend" Mizell pitched well for us in 1960, gave us that boost that we needed. "Vinegar Bend" won 13 games for us. Clem Labine won some big ballgames in relief.

*   *   *   *   *

Celebrating a 1960 World Series victory with ElRoy Face

Bottom of the 9th, seventh game of the '60 Series, we were just hoping somebody would get on and get a rally going. That's what Maz was trying to do. But when Ralph Terry laid that ball up there belt high for him, Maz just smacked it. Maz had done that before. He'd become a pretty darn good clutch hitter for us. Two outs, couple of men on, he would come through and get a base hit. He had done that several times. We had confidence in Maz up there.

And Maz was unbelievable in the field. The thing that made him so good was he would get such a jump on the ball. He would get to balls that a lot of guys wouldn't because he was so quick with that first step. Maz was not afraid to lay himself out to get a ball either. I've seen him in a prone position fielding the ball. A lot of guys won't do that. Don't want to get their uniform dirty, I guess. Maz would constantly come up with balls we thought were base hits. You're running over to back up a base and here Maz has got the ball and he's throwing that hitter out!

When I visualize his double plays, the ball just takes a turn. It doesn't ever seem to stop. Just makes a bend and goes on to first base. That's how quick he would be at getting rid of the ball. I have never seen anybody quicker, getting it out of the glove and on its way to first.

I saw a lot of second basemen and Maz was the best. He didn't say a heck of a lot on the field. He was not a holler guy. Maz let his glove and his bat do the speaking for him and that was good enough for me.

* * * * *

I hurt my arm late in 1960. It was miserable for about four years. People thought my career was over but I liked the game too much to quit. I didn't have enough sense to quit. Murtaugh told me, "Deacon, if I were you, I would go home and forget it. You've had such a good career I'd hate to see you diminish it." In the winter of '63, I was home trying to learn new pitches, trying to stay in the big leagues.

I went to Salt Lake City to speak at a youth conference. Afterwards, I met with some of the general authorities of the church and they gave me a blessing. In our church, we believe that through our faith and the authority that the priesthood holds, miracles can be performed. People can be healed. I went home, picked up a baseball and I knew my arm was all right. When I threw, I heard something pop, and I threw again. It felt good, there was no pain for the first time.

From that point on, in the '64 season I did okay and I feel my '65 season was my best one in baseball. I could have won every game that I pitched.

* * * * *

Maz should be in the Hall of Fame. There are guys who get in for hitting home runs, some get in for batting average, why not get in for fielding the ball, turning double plays and being a great infielder?

Bill made all the plays in the field and turned so many double plays to save a lot of runs. A run saved is like a run made. Maz has done as much for baseball as anyone, not just because he hit the Series-winning home run in 1960 but because of the way he handled himself on the field. Fans would really enjoy watching him play. He would give you a thrill a minute out there if you could just make the ball go his way.

It was fun, as a player, to watch him from the bench, playing this difficult game, day in and day out. You just didn't believe some of the things that he would do.

I have to mention Bill's wife Milene, too. She's a real supporter. Baseball is a tough, tough life for a wife. People think it's all glamour; the heck it is. Baseball can be really tough on a family and if you don't have the right kind of wife who can handle it then, boy, life is miserable. After I met Milene, I said Maz, she's the kind of girl you need. And she was.

"Maz played with pain. I was his room-mate and I saw how bruised his legs were. But I never, never heard him complain."

– "Vinegar Bend" Mizell

9

"Vinegar Bend" Mizell

Wilmer "Vinegar Bend" Mizell was a hard-throwing left-hander who broke in with the Cardinals in 1952. After military service in '56 and '57, Mizell resumed pitching for St. Louis. In May, 1960, Mizell was traded to the Pirates for Julian Javier and Ed Bauta. Mizell was 13-5 for Pittsburgh in 1960; with southpaw Harvey Haddix he complemented righthanders Bob Friend and Vernon Law in a formidable starting rotation. In spring '62, Mizell was traded to the Mets; their first year was his last in the majors. Mizell's career totals are 90 wins, including 15 shutouts, and 88 losses, with a 3.85 E.R.A. A three-term U.S. congressman from North Carolina, 1969-1975, "Vinegar Bend" is active with the Christian Missionary Alliance Church.

M az was so quick with that double play. He would come across that bag and the ball just turned the corner right over to first base. Maz and I roomed together on the road when I came over from the Cardinals. Maz was beginning to receive recognition because of his outstanding play in the field, but he was a good hitter too. Good in the clutch, and unaffected by the notoriety he was getting.

Maz came from kind of a meager background. Mine was similar, coming from Vinegar Bend. Without baseball, who knows what Maz would have been doing, who knows what I might have been doing? I might have still been plowing that mule down in Vinegar Bend, where I spent many a hot summer day.

Maz was kind of quiet. But he loved to talk about hunting and fishing, his deer-hunting trips in the wintertime. Living out in the country where I did, you walk out your front gate, you were already hunting.

* * * * *

I was born in 1930 in Greene County in Leakesville, Mississippi, but we lived out in the country. Our home address was always Route One, Vinegar Bend, Alabama. Our field fence ran right up the Mississippi-Alabama line where I used to plow with that old mule. It was a miracle I even got to play baseball. We didn't have a baseball team in high school, didn't have any of the programs they do today.

We organized us a team. Living out in the country it was just about all family. The first year we played two games. Next season we got some uniforms. The Long Branch Rebels' baseball diamond was in the corner of a cow pasture.

Uncle Irvan was the coach of the team; he also played third base. Uncle Fletcher would umpire. And don't forget Uncle Buck. We played for two seasons and became a pretty good bunch of knockers and stoppers.

The way I happened to play pro ball involved a St. Louis Cardinals' tryout camp in Biloxi. Six of us loaded up in a little automobile and went down. Must have been 1,000 boys in that camp, from all over the South. Everybody had a number.

I was the last pitcher of the day. I got to the pitcher's mound about 4:30. They brought my brother in to catch. I threw nine pitches and struck out three men. That's all the scouts saw me pitch. They called the camp off for the day; that night there was a hurricane bouncing around in the Gulf. Rained so hard the next morning they had to call the camp off. Buddy Lewis was the scout in charge.

Next spring, the day I graduated from high school, Buddy Lewis showed up in Vinegar Bend and got someone to bring him out to the country, where we lived. My first cousin and I were getting our baths to go to graduation exercises, down in the swim hole. We got out and by the time we got back to the house, Buddy said, "I'd just like to see you warm up." My brother caught for me, about five or ten minutes or so, then Buddy said, "I'd like you to go to Albany, Georgia and pitch Class D baseball this summer – if you will, I've got a contract for you, $175.00 per month." I didn't know what to say to Buddy. This was a surprise. In those days scouts didn't talk to high school boys, so I hadn't heard anything from Buddy over the winter other than a Christmas card. Buddy must have thought I was holding out on him – he said, "Well, when you get to Albany, Georgia, I'll see that they give you $500.00." I almost broke his arm getting the pen to sign that contract. Uncle Irvan had to sign for me. I was still underage. He put me on a train that night to Albany, Georgia. I didn't even go home after graduation exercises.

My first game, we were getting beat 15-0, and Hal Smith was our catcher. About 2500 people in that little ballpark. Smitty gives me a sign. Fastball. He knew that was the only pitch I threw. I turned that first pitch loose and hit the back-stop, 20 feet high. Next pitch was a foot behind the batter's head; he went sprawling on home plate. Smitty told me later after he and I had both made it to the Cardinals, "I was just as nervous as I could be that night, until I realized I was the safest man in the ballpark."

* * * * *

Harley Bowers, a sports editor for the *Albany Herald,* wrote about the big left-hander from Vinegar Bend, Alabama. The next thing I know, they were saying "Vinegar Bend" will be starting tonight. That name had been given to the town years ago, when one of Vinegar Bend's staples was sorghum molasses. Seems there was a barrel of molasses that went sour and was emptied into the bend of the Escatawba River.

When I got to Albany, Georgia, I had been used to getting up early. Suddenly you're playing night games. I would stay in bed as long as I could and still get up early and walk down the street in Albany. Everything would be closed. There was only one other person awake, in the old livery stable on the bank of the Flint River; I would walk down there, sit on a bale of hay and talk to him till breakfast. This homesick boy had never been away from the farm. Luckily Uncle Irvan and of course my cousins, Rooster and Goat Wallace, my brother Curtis, they all got in an old car and came to see me. I'm telling you, that did me more good than anything else!

The next year in Winston-Salem, for Player Appreciation Night, the ballclub wanted me to ride a mule in from center field, get off at home plate, and sing "Country Boy." Nobody knew if the mule had been ridden before. Only one way to find out. I got on the mule, rode in, sang "Country Boy," and pitched the ballgame. Won it 1-0.

Nobody had ever tried to show me anything. My high-kick delivery was a natural delivery that I used all the time. And strikeouts just happened. I struck out 18 one game in Albany, Georgia. Later on, I struck out 18 in Winston-Salem one night. Struck out 18 in the Texas League, too. But the most I ever struck out in the big leagues in one game was 14.

We had good teams with the Cardinals, with players like Red Schoendienst, Enos Slaughter, Stan Musial, and later Ken Boyer. In 1959, I slipped on the pitcher's mound just before the All-Star game. I was 10-2. We had a sudden downpour, they didn't get the pitcher's mound covered. When I went back out, on the first pitch I made, my foot slipped out from under me. Man, I felt things pull from my hips to my shoulders. I went on to pitch about seven innings. The next day I got muscle spasms, the kind that squeeze the breath out of you.

I struggled through the next spring training. In 1960 I was 1-3 with the Cardinals and the day before the trading deadline, I was pitching against Milwaukee's great team; for the first time since I'd slipped on that pitcher's mound, I felt good. Popping that ball with good control, my good breaking ball and good fastball back, I struck out 10 in seven innings. St. Louis then traded me to Pittsburgh.

All my teammates on the Pirates have been more than generous as to my contribution in 1960. I won 13 ballgames, but I was there just a short time. Bob Friend, Vernon Law, and Harvey Haddix were the established starters.

Mazeroski was a bright spot on that club. Here was a young fellow with real fielding skill. And he was not an easy out for a left-handed pitcher. One time with St. Louis I intentionally threw him a fastball up. After that, anything up was a mistake. And it took playing on the Pirates for me to recognize how well Maz anchored that second base bag.

1960: "Starting pitcher in a World Series game"

1960 turned out to be the happiest and best season I ever spent in baseball. One ambition that I wanted to accomplish before I left baseball was to be a starting pitcher in a World Series game. Game 3 of the World Series in New York City, we entered Yankee Stadium with 65,000 people on hand and 40 million watching on television. I was the starting pitcher for the Pirates. If you didn't turn it on early, you missed me. I laugh about it now, but it wasn't funny at the time.

I came back in the sixth game and pitched two hitless innings. In the seventh game, if Maz doesn't hit that home run, I was already warmed up in the bullpen. I was on my way to the dugout, underneath the stands; there was a television down there. I was in front of the T.V. when Maz hit the home run. Never did get to the dugout. I think I was the only Pirate who didn't see the home run on the field. I'll have to say I was glad I didn't have to pitch any more. What an exciting time. Nobody could get out of town until the next day!

Looking back, we had a terrific fielding ballclub in 1960. Bill Virdon made one of the greatest catches that year that I ever saw. I was pitching against the Giants. Even though Virdon made many fine catches, you remember those he made for you more than those he made for other pitchers. It was 1-0, eighth or ninth inning, someone was on first base, two out. The shortstop hit the ball to deep left center field. Bill Virdon went into that wall, put his cleats in that ivy, leapt and caught the ball. I don't know how he made such a play. That was the ballgame.

In another close game that season, someone hit a looping line drive to right field. Roberto Clemente went into the wall, sliced his chin on the concrete and came away with the ball. Roberto took quite a lick but he caught that ball. And of course I can still visualize the double plays that Maz turned.

I don't know why there was never a no-hitter pitched in Forbes Field. You might blame that on the hard ground around home plate; balls would bounce high. Clemente used his speed to get a few hits that way. There weren't very many no-hitters thrown in my day. Today it seems like the hitter is on the end of the bat. Whether he has one strike or two strikes on him, he's swinging from his heels. Somebody doing that is not hard to pitch to. If you had two strikes on a hitter in my day, he guarded that plate.

*   *   *   *   *

Nobody else could have used a glove like Maz's. Bill was so sure-handed that he could use a dinky little glove; I never saw a ball get stuck in it. Maz had unusual skills. If Groat got that ball to Maz, you'd know it was a double play. That ball turning the corner at second base was something to see. Bill had real strong legs, so even if that runner was right on him, he made the play. I can't remember when a runner took him out. If he had to, just to make that double play, Bill would let a runner come into him.

Maz played with pain. I was his roommate and I saw how bruised his legs were. But I never, never heard him complain. And how he loved to go to the ballpark. He was there to play hard.

How would I describe Maz to a casual fan? I would say, "Hey, I want you to meet Bill Mazeroski, the greatest double play man that ever played behind me when I was pitching." To prove it, he holds the record in double plays. Bill is a man of character, principle. Bill was able to make a commitment to the game, to his teammates and to his family – and I really mean that. One more thing. Bill was a great roommate on the road.

*"**A**ny time you were in trouble, you just hoped the batter would hit the ball to Maz."*

– ElRoy Face

10

ElRoy Face

Master of the forkball, ElRoy Face pitched for the Pittsburgh Pirates in 1953 and 1955-68, the Tigers in 1968, and the Expos in 1969. ElRoy was a three-time All-Star (1959, 1960, 1961); he set a major league record with twenty-two consecutive wins in relief – his last five decisions in 1958 and first seventeen in 1959. The premier relief pitcher of the late '50s and early '60s, Face's 18-1 winning percentage (.947) in 1959 is also a major league record.

I was sixteen years old in high school in New York state before I ever played ball. We had no Little League or anything where I lived. When we won the high school championship it was the first time any team of the school ever won a championship. I quit school when I was eighteen and joined the Army. Spent a year and a half in the service. I was on a team and we would call another town and if they weren't playing that Sunday, we would either go to their field or they would come over to our field and play. I had consecutive games when I struck out seventeen and eighteen batters. A scout on vacation for the Phillies read about it in the paper, came over and watched me pitch a ballgame on Labor Day, 1948. In the seventh inning, he signed me up to a contract.

I was twenty at that time; the next year I was in Class D: Bradford, Pennsylvania in the Phillies organization. Played with them two years and then was drafted by the Dodgers – Branch Rickey drafted me. The year he drafted me, he came to Pittsburgh. Two years later Mr. Rickey drafted me for Pittsburgh.

I was two years in Class D. Got drafted and went to Class A in Pueblo, Colorado. Then Double A in Ft. Worth, Texas, in '52. Finally I was drafted by Pittsburgh and came there in '53.

That was my biggest break, coming to Pittsburgh, because I had belonged to the Dodgers and they had Don Newcombe and Spooner and Preacher Roe and Erskine and Labine – no way I was going to break into that pitching rotation. Pittsburgh was rebuilding: the year before they had lost 112 ballgames.

In '53 when I came up as a starting pitcher, I had a fastball and a curveball. Mr. Rickey wanted me to go down to New Orleans and work on an off-speed pitch. So I was sent back to New Orleans. That spring Joe Page was trying a comeback with the Pirates; he threw the forkball. I watched him in spring training, saw what it was doing for him, and when I got to New Orleans that's when I started working on the forkball. I developed that pitch, worked on it for about one-half season, started using it, then came back to the Pirates in '55.

I think I was the only one at that time throwing it. They used to accuse me of throwing a spitball, because it would sink.

If it was working I might use it sixty or seventy percent of the time. If it wasn't, I may have used it twenty percent.

But I would throw it on any count – three and two, or three and one – it wouldn't make any difference. If I got them looking for that, then I could throw the fastball by them and if they were looking for the fastball, they'd be out in front of the forkball.

* * * * *

I was a pretty good fielder, too. Lee Walls was with Pittsburgh early in the '50s, then he went to the Cubs; I was pitching one day at Forbes Field and he tried to bunt one down the third base line. I went over, got it and threw him out. After the game he said he had forgotten who was pitching. He knew I was a good fielder – I never won any Gold Gloves, but most are won by starting pitchers anyway.

Another thing I'd be doing, that they don't concentrate enough on now, is holding runners close. I had a good move to second and to first – I came in a game in Cincinnati one night with men on first and second and nobody out – picked the guy off second, then picked the guy off first, before I pitched to a batter! I had two outs, nobody on, when there had been two on and nobody out. Another time against Orlando Cepeda, I threw over six straight times to first base without pitching to the batter. Jim Marshall was playing first base; I threw over the seventh time and Cepeda was out by eight feet. After the inning, Marshall told me, "I'm glad you came over there because he had his mind made up to steal second base."

Groat and I used the daylight play at second base quite a bit: one time Curt Simmons came in to pinch-run, for the Cardinals. That was in '60 when we were neck and neck with the Cardinals in mid-July. The daylight play happens when the runner takes his lead; the shortstop comes in behind him and then he starts to back up; as that runner starts to take a step more on his lead, the shortstop breaks to second base. If you can see daylight between the shortstop and the runner, nine times out of ten you're going to get your runner, because he is taking a step toward third and your shortstop is already breaking to second base. We had plays where when your hands come together in a stretch, count 1001, 1002, 1003 and turn to throw. When the shortstop, or second baseman, sees your hands come together he does the same thing – counts to 1001, then breaks on 1002; you turn and throw on 1003. The fielder should be at the bag. Also, the center fielder knows the sign that the pickoff play's on – so he can come in a bit in case the ball is thrown through.

When you come in to pitch in a ballgame, you've got to know the situation of the game, the runners on base: Are they fast or slow? You've got to know if the ball comes back to you, is the guy on first a sure out at second, or too fast, or are you going to have to throw to first, to make sure the first baseman gets the batter. A lot on your mind.

At the same time, you concentrate on where you're throwing the ball and what type of pitches you're throwing.

I won a game in Chicago. Man on first, two outs and Billy Williams the hitter. I had two balls and one strike on Williams. I made a pitch and Billy took it for a strike. So now I had two and two on him. Our catcher, Jim Pagliaroni, came out to me and said, "You know that guy on first?" I said, "Yeah." Jim said, "He's on second now." I looked and said, "How did he get there?" I didn't realize I had wound up. As it happened, Williams popped up on the next pitch.

But when I got in the dugout Murtaugh said to me, "What are you thinking about out there?" I said, "That's the only way I could get Williams to take a strike." But I didn't realize that I had wound up. I was so involved in the game. With men on base, I always pitched from the stretch. But I just happened to wind up that time instead of pitching from the stretch; that runner just walked to second base.

Murtaugh was good to play for because if you did your job he just left you alone. If you didn't, he let you know. He knew his players, the ones he had to pat on the back to get the most out of, and the ones to kick in the butt. He knew everything about them, on and off the field.

One time in L.A., Groat went deep in the hole between third and short. Dick Stuart at first base thought it was going to be a base hit, so he turned around and talked to the umpire. Groat got to the ball, threw it to first and it went right by Dick's ear – he had his back turned!

Winning or tying run on first base, it wouldn't make any difference, I'd come in from the bullpen in right field and Stuart would kick the dirt, work his way over and I would have to walk by him. "Don't throw to me, I don't want to foul up anymore." Dick's a good guy. He'd poke fun at himself.

I've seen a ball that Musial hit just by Stuart at first base, and Maz went over on the outfield grass, dove and got it and threw it from his knees – threw Musial out at first base.

Just the other night at second base, the fielder dove, got the ball and turned around on his knees to throw the guy out at second base. Night before last on TV. Maz did it all the time.

I don't remember Maz getting taken out on a double play – getting hit. He always avoided it. Maz's double play was like an elbow on a stove pipe – the ball comes in one side and out the other side. It never stops. I mean get it and it's gone. He had quick hands.

* * * * *

My first All-Star Game, the American League was loosening up for their infield practice in front of the third base dugout. As we started our infield, they all stopped throwing.

They just stood there and watched Maz make the double play because they hadn't seen him – but they'd heard about him. They stood there in amazement. Maz even today says it embarrassed him a little bit, all those guys watching him.

He could do it. Without a doubt, he should be in the Hall of Fame. They've got Aparicio in there. Maz probably broke just about all the fielding records Jackie Robinson held and Jackie is in the Hall of Fame. If Maz had played for the Dodgers or Cardinals or a New York team, he'd be in there. Playing in Pittsburgh you didn't get publicity.

Think about Joe Morgan...Harry Walker told me that he had brought Maz in to show Morgan how to do the double play. Joe was getting hurt by opening up his left side. Maz helped Joe immensely there.

Everybody looked up to Maz. If you'd go to him with a problem, he'd try to help you out. Only if you asked him – otherwise he wouldn't butt in.

Hal Smith, Haddix, Maz and me, we'd play cards in the clubhouse and drink a couple of beers – we'd just sit and talk about the game and certain plays and things like that. They say now that twenty minutes after the game there's nobody left in a clubhouse. We used to sit there sometimes an hour or two hours after a game.

There was togetherness. We'd get six or eight guys together and go out to eat together. Now they don't do it. They go their own directions. Go research their bank accounts.

My first major league manager? Fred Haney. Fred did not have much to work with. When I came to Pittsburgh, there was a bunch of young kids and they were trying to rebuild.

Then Bragan took over in '56; I had played for him in '52 at Ft. Worth. He knew what I could do and wanted to see the other pitchers. So in spring training I didn't make any road trips. I'd started for Bobby in Ft. Worth and I would come in between starts to pitch an inning or two in relief, take a day's rest, come back in and throw a couple of innings in relief if I had to. Then get another day's rest and start every fourth day. He knew that I had a good arm and that I could recuperate quickly. I started six or seven games in '56. I was supposed to start one in '57 in Chicago, the day Bragan was fired, but Murtaugh took over, scratched me and put me in the bullpen. I never started another game.

Branch Rickey drafted me to the Dodgers and then two years later drafted me to Pittsburgh. I guess he saw something nobody else saw. When I first came up, I got married. Mr. Rickey was the first one we went to see after we got married. We went to his office. He loved anybody that got married. He'd rather have them married than single.

Al Leap was our shortstop at Pueblo, I think in '51. Mr. Rickey wanted him to get married. He told him, "If you get married I'll take you downtown...pick out a car you like and I will buy it for you." Al went to Mr. Rickey and told him he'd found a girlfriend and he was getting married.

Rickey said, "That's great." Al went downtown and picked

out this Ford convertible. He had it in '51. Mr. Rickey bought Leap the car and Al never got married!

Once Bob Friend wanted a raise, went to see Mr. Rickey and while there, I guess Rickey had his son call on the phone in his office like he was a minor league manager. Mr. Rickey said, "Well I've got some guys you could probably have down there this year." He said to Bobby, "You signed your contract?" Bobby said, "Yes, Mr. Rickey." Friend was going in there to get a raise, but after he overheard this phony conversation, it was, "Yes, Mr. Rickey, I signed it. It's right here in my pocket."

Ralph Kiner went in after we lost 112 ballgames in '52. Kiner had hit maybe forty home runs, and he wanted a raise. Mr. Rickey said, "Where did we finish?" Kiner said, "Last." Rickey said, "Well, we can finish last without you." Kiner never got his raise.

* * * * *

I think the major leagues are a lot thinner than when we had eight teams to a league, just sixteen teams. The National League has two more teams in Miami and Denver – that's fifty more minor leaguers playing in the big leagues. When I came up with the Dodgers, you had Pee Wee Reese, Robinson, Hodges, Snider, Furillo, Campanella – an awesome lineup. Now you have one guy to worry about. The rest are outs.

Lots of pitchers now are groomed right from the minor leagues just for relief. When I played, guys who relieved were mostly guys who maybe couldn't go nine innings. Teams did not have anyone else to bring up, so they kept them and put them in the bullpen.

In Montreal, playing for Gene Mauch, the Giants got the bases loaded with nobody out in the first inning. Mauch brought me in. We got out of the inning. They scored one run, so we were down 1-0 in the first inning. The next inning he pinch-hit for me. After the game he called me in his office and said, "Do you have any idea why I did that?" I said, "I think it was a tough situation." Mauch told me, "You can save a game as much in the first inning as you can in the ninth." He said, "If they score four or five runs, now we've got to get six to catch 'em. You stopped 'em, so we only need two runs to win." That was the only time I went in before the seventh inning.

I'd pitch in a lot of games. Seventy-two games total in 1960. In that era, you were going in the seventh inning and maybe pitching three or four innings at a time – you weren't just pitching to one or two batters in the ninth inning as you do now.

With the Pirates I was lucky to have Bill Virdon in center field; he could go get that ball. I would rather have him in center field than Mays or anybody. He could go back real well and come in. When a ball was hit, he just took off. When he turned around, he was where the ball was. Virdon didn't make spectacular catches. He made everything look routine.

I was with Clemente fourteen years, '55 until '68. With Maz, thirteen years. These days the good players spend a couple of years with one club and then some other club will offer them another million, and they're gone – free agency. When we played, if you didn't sign a contract, you didn't put a uniform on in spring training. You couldn't work out. Now they can play all year without a contract, earning a percentage of what they made the year before.

* * * * *

I mostly watch baseball on television now. I don't go down to the ballpark much. Unless there's something going on and the Pirates want us down there. We incorporated the Pirates' Alumni. Money that we raise we donate to charities in the area – Children's Hospital, Cancer Fund, the Sharing Program, different things – $1000 here, $3000 there.

1959? We had good offense when we needed it. That year I went 18-1. I could have lost five or six games, but we would tie it up and I won them. I think I pitched better ball in '60 than in '59. 1960 was one of those years where everything went right.

After we won the '60 Series, I guess it was a pretty good civic celebration. I didn't see much of it because we went to Webster Hall for a private party for the players, which the ball club gave us. So I never got downtown, and Maz and I and Smoky Burgess had to leave the next morning and drive to New Jersey for an exhibition game – a National League team against an American League team. We played in New Jersey, then Syracuse and Utica. So we weren't out too late that evening.

Back to 1959: the Esso station across the street from Gustine's where we'd park usually charged us $1.00 a day. When I was about four or five wins without a loss, Bud, the owner, said he wouldn't charge me until I lost. So I didn't have to pay for parking until September!

That same year, during Haddix's 12-inning perfect game that he lost in the 13th, I never went to the bullpen – just sat and watched the whole game from the bench. You could tell he was throwing freely and putting the ball where he wanted to all the time – mixing his pitches up well. Just the greatest game ever pitched! Were we pretending it wasn't happening, trying not to jinx him? Well, I couldn't say. There are twenty-five guys on a club; maybe someone mentioned it. I couldn't say.

Fifth game of the 1960 World Series: Face earns his third save of the Series

The other relievers around the league? Lindy McDaniel was really good, as were a number of them. I admired their ability, although I was rooting against them. McDaniel would come over to me in batting practice, asking how I threw the forkball. I would show him. Then he started working on it and using it.

The All-Star Game in '59...that was my first time on the All-Star team. I was on in '60 and '61, but '59 was not a very good showing! With the bases loaded, I gave up a double and three runs scored. It would have been my first loss that year. The National League came back to win. I faced Ted Williams and ended up walking him the only time I ever faced him. If Ted didn't swing at a pitch, the umpire figured it must have been a ball.

* * * * *

My routine during a game was to go back and forth in the clubhouse. Sometimes I'd lie down, sometimes fall asleep and they'd have to come in at the seventh inning and wake me up and tell me to get warmed up. I knew I wasn't going to pitch before the seventh.

Walter Johnson and I share the record of 802 appearances with the same team. Nobody will ever match that now because of free agency – nobody stays with a team long enough to get it.

In '65 I was operated on, had a cartilage removed from my right knee and only got in eighteen games that year. Other than that, I'd have been maybe eight hundred and fifty ballgames with one club. I never had a sore arm.

I'd get a little bit tired at times. In '56 I pitched in nine straight ballgames. At times the arm was tired and throbbing when I'd go to bed, but when I'd wake up, I felt like I hadn't pitched in a week. Never packed it in ice, like some do. Never babied it. I'd go out and warm up and in about two or three pitches I was throwing as hard as I could throw.

Toughest hitters...when I first came up, Richie Ashburn gave me a lot of trouble; he's a broadcaster with the Phillies. [Ashburn was inducted into baseball's Hall of Fame in July,

1995.] Ironically he once said I was the toughest pitcher he had ever faced! The big hitters like Mays, Aaron, Mathews and Musial – they got their hits. I know Musial beat me in a ballgame in St. Louis one night in the tenth inning, but I did not have that much trouble with the big hitters. It was the little guys like the Ashburns, the Matty Alous, spraying the ball around.

Getting back to Maz...I first met him in '56. Right away you could tell he had good hands. We played together from '56 to '68. Any time you were in trouble, you just hoped the batter would hit the ball to Maz.

*"**M**r. Rickey knew Maz was something special. Branch Rickey could judge talent."*

– Nellie King

11

Nellie King

Nellie King has the unusual perspective of playing with Bill Mazeroski (as a Pirate pitcher in the mid-'50s), and later covering him from the Pirates' broadcast booth.

Maz turned the double play better than anybody in the history of baseball. If you're a pitcher, you throw one ball and you get two outs.

Ask any pitcher if he should be in the Hall of Fame, he'll say, yeah. Ask any manager who saw him play, and he'll say, yeah. Now, sportswriters, they have no knowledge of that part of the game.

I know Maz and he comes off with that Polish guy thing, like, "I'm not too smart." One of his kids is a very intelligent computer expert, and he didn't lick it off the grass. Maz is very intelligent.

Everybody looks at a guy and says: "Yeah, he's a natural athlete. He just goes out and plays. He doesn't have to work out." Michael Jordan in basketball, Bill Mazeroski, they spent eight hours a day becoming a natural athlete, practicing what they do. The work to get to that level is unbelievable.

Maz said the greatest coach he ever had was his high school coach, Al Burazio. They used to play catch with a tennis ball. You can't catch a tennis ball with one hand.

It's going to pop out because you can't feel it. It's not hard, so it's not going to go into the glove. You have to learn to feel for it. If you play with a tennis ball, you get away from the fear of the ball and you learn how to catch and how to feel for the ball. You get confidence.

Everybody thinks players don't have fears. Maz says when he was young he was afraid of the ball. It was going to hit him. Guys will tell you, "Get down and get your nose down there. The ball won't hurt you." Hell, one will knock your teeth out. You may lose an eye if you get hit with the ball, or break your nose, certainly.

Maz says Burazio told him, "Hey, instead of playing the ball head on, why don't you play it off the shoulder? If you play it off this [right] shoulder, you don't have to worry about it, and when you field it, you're ready to throw anyway." That's what he always did. He always played it off this shoulder and he was so quick throwing the ball.

Ted Williams said the best thing he ever did when he was younger – eighteen or nineteen – was playing with guys who were thirty. Guys like that had wisdom. They can tell you

what to do. When you're a teenager, you don't know anything. Good players play with older players. Maz had talent
and he was ready to play when he came up because he knew
something about the game. Maz had played in the mine
leagues in Ohio.

*   *   *   *   *

I went to a boys' school, the Milton Hershey School in
Hershey, Pennsylvania. They didn't have a baseball team. We
lived on farms, and had to work – get up at 5:30 in the morning, milk cows, work in the fields all day, then go play baseball.

I wasn't physically developed when I came out of high
school, so I spent a year playing YMCA ball in 1945. I had
turned seventeen in March, I was six foot five and weighed
around a hundred and fifty. A real bean pole.

But I got stronger the next year; I was pitching in a youth
league. There was a guy who ran a machine shop, Jimmy
Kercher; we had his name on the back of our uniforms. He
was our coach. Just a machine shop. But that gave me an
opportunity to play baseball.

And so a Cardinal scout saw me. Charlie Kelschner signed
me to a contract. It was the greatest thing that could ever
happen. I got a hundred dollars a month. In '45 or '46, I
went to Albany, Georgia, was there two weeks and got
released.

I came home, was working at the Bethlehem Steel plant in
Lebanon, and there was a tryout camp at Fredericksburg,
Pennsylvania, where Kenny Boyer started, playing Class D ball.
That's where I went in July, 1946, me and three other kids from
our YMCA league. We hitchhiked twelve or fifteen miles with
our bats and gloves and spikes and baseball uniforms. And I
had a hell of a day. Roy Dissinger had been a Cardinal scout
and he knew Kelschner. He signed me right there. No bonus –
he was going to give me a hundred and twenty-five a month.
They sent me to New Iberia, Louisiana. God.

But I get down there, in '46, with all these guys coming out
of the service: that league was full of old ballplayers. Guys

twenty-eight to thirty years old, playing Class D baseball. I was there two weeks and got released again. So in one year I got two tickets.

The next year, Dissinger offers me a contract to go to the New Orleans farm team's spring training camp in Anderson, South Carolina. The last day he comes up to look at players: "We're going to check them off and see who's going to make the teams." To get a good look at pitchers, instead of staying out there for one inning getting three outs, you stayed out until you got six or nine outs.

I gave up a hit, got two outs, another big hit, got one third out, and then it was a double, a single, we get an out, then a triple. Another guy hit a double, and I knew this was all over.

The length of a football field was where the locker room was. And I'm almost sobbing because I know I'm going back to Lebanon, PA. I said a silent prayer. They start calling names for the teams. Geneva, Alabama: so and so, and so and so, and then, "King." I could tell all the players were saying, "Him?"

The change in my life in the minor leagues was playing with older guys. I could throw strikes. I had great control. Cotton Bosarge played second base for us. He must have been twenty-six or twenty-seven, playing Class D ball in Geneva, Alabama. Population twenty-five hundred, counting everything that moves. Cotton was watching me pitch. "You know," he says, "you've got good control." "You've got a nice delivery," he said, "But your ball doesn't move at all." Cotton asked, "How do you hold your fastball?" "I hold it across the seams." "Why do you do that?" "Well, I read in the book that's the way Bob Feller throws his fastball." To which Cotton replied, "Hell, you can't throw as hard as Bob Feller."

"You know you've got to make a ball move. If you throw it that way, it's going to rise. Why don't you turn it over and hold it this way? You throw out of here and it'll sink. It'll run in for you."

Bang. That year, 1947, I finished the season there and they brought me up to Anderson, Class B ball, to see if they could get in the playoffs. The next year I went back to New Iberia, where I'd been released the year before, with this pitch. I won twenty games, pitching two hundred and ninety innings.

If not for Bosarge, I'm still holding the ball and they'd say, "Hey, this guy doesn't have anything. His fastball doesn't work. Get rid of him."

The next year, I went to spring training in New Orleans. Didn't make the team. Went to York, Pennsylvania, led that league in pitching. The next year I went to Charleston, South Carolina. We used to go out to Folly Beach in the morning and ride waves. I wondered why I had a bad year...I was always out at the goddamn beach in the morning and I'd come back in the afternoon, take a nap and not pitch too well.

Spent 1951 and 1952 in the Army and pitched some ball there. We had a decent team at Fort Dix. Harvey Haddix was on that team, Don McMahon, Frank Torre.

Look at those events – a guy like Roy Dissinger. Why in the hell did he pick me out of that crowd that day? Why Cotton Bosarge? I had good stuff. I could throw in the low eighties. Had a good sinker and could throw strikes.

Denver the next year, 1953, had a 2.00 E.R.A., led the league at 15-3. I relieved mostly, and I had fifteen, sixteen saves.

Then the Pirates' General Manager, Branch Rickey, came out and I did a personal audition for him. I got to the big leagues in '53. The day I got married was October 10th, 1953; I picked up the *New York Times* on our honeymoon, October 11th, and saw in Transactions, "Pirates purchase the contract of Nelson King from Denver." At least my wife was a major leaguer from the start.

I didn't make it in '54. I should have played. It would hurt me, not getting on the pension plan. But they had to carry two bonus players, both catchers. They were carrying four catchers and these two guys couldn't catch anything, but they had bonuses. If they were paid a bonus of more than five thousand, they'd have to stay on the major league roster.

I got sent down after a month and I had a good spring training. I wasn't young, I had spent seven years in the minors, counting two in the Army, and I hadn't been in the big leagues yet because I had to struggle to get up there. I did not exactly knock anybody's eyes out throwing the ball hard but I knew how to pitch, I could throw strikes, and I didn't walk anybody.

Andy Cohen was my manager at Denver, and in 1954 in spring training, he was at the major league camp. I was having a good spring. "They like what you're doing," Andy said, "but keep having a good day because they're looking for a reason to send you out." That's the way it was.

I went down to New Orleans and had a hell of a year, led that league in E.R.A. I was pitching well as a starter. Then they began using me in relief because they'd need a save and I could throw strikes in late innings. I'd start, too, and my arm got tired. The next year I didn't have much.

* * * * *

I met Maz in spring training in '55. Mr. Rickey knew Maz was something special. Branch Rickey could judge talent. Maz wore a porkpie hat, he was a little guy, only eighteen or nineteen. That's the first time I remember seeing him. Maz would come up in '56. They didn't have anyone who could turn a double play. They'd tried Curt Roberts, Spook Jacobs.

[Pirates' manager] Bobby Bragan would drive you crazy though, because he was always thinking of ways to win today. He wasn't worried about two years down the road. He'd start Maz and take him out for a pinch hitter in the second inning! He did that a couple of times. Maz never batted in the ballgame. He started. Got taken out because we had a runner in scoring position. I was the short reliever that year, '56.

I played winter ball in Mexico in Mazatlan after the '55 season, to try to get my breaking ball back. We opened the season in Los Mochis and they had a hurricane hit the coast before we came down.

I'd ridden a lot of buses in the minor leagues. We come to a river. "Everybody get out." Get our luggage, get in a rowboat, and we go across the river in a rowboat! We did that twice. I felt like George Washington going across the Delaware, with the equipment, to get to Los Mochis!

Got there and no grass on the field at all. All sand. I'm

feeling really bad – dysentery. I'm pitching and I get up to the fourth inning, sitting in the dugout and I see this thing, looks like a balloon, rolling across the field, only it's pigs' intestines that somebody blew up, veins still on it, blood coming out, picking up dirt as it rolls. I got sicker.

* * * * *

Anyway that next year, '56, we were in first place in June. ElRoy Face was the long relief. He's five seven and I'm six six. I was pitching short relief and ElRoy was the long relief.

One game that season I relieved ElRoy when the Cubs had us down 8-5 with two outs in the top of the ninth. On the first pitch I got Eddie Miksis to ground out to Groat at short.

Bottom of the ninth against Turk Lown, nobody out, we load the bases. Jim Brosnan comes in to pitch to Roberto Clemente. Roberto hits the first pitch to left center field; the ball bounces off the light tower and caroms to center. Roberto beats the throw home for an inside-the-park grand slam, and we win 9-8!

That was one of my seven wins in the big leagues. Brosnan lost, I won. We each threw one pitch. Now that's short relief!

Later in June, I was pitching against the Cubs' Gene Baker, threw him a curveball and Christ, my arm hurt. Wow. I should have walked off. But you've got to gut it out. Dee Fondy comes up. I said, "I can't throw a curveball. I'll throw a fastball." I threw a fastball and it still hurt. That was the last time I threw without pain.

The major leagues are a tough place to pitch if you're healthy. And if you're not healthy, you're like a wounded deer with wolves around. They'll get you.

In '57, I tried to pitch again, and it got worse and worse. The Pirates released me. The only misgiving I have is I missed the damn pension plan. I didn't get anything – you had to have five years.

I tried to sell investments. I hated calling people up, "Will you give me two thousand?" I tried to sell municipal bonds. Caddied at a country club. Worked at liquor stores in the wintertime.

Finally something opened in radio, at a small station in Kittanning, then Latrobe and Greensburg, Pennsylvania. I covered golf, went to the Masters, the Open, the PGA, when Arnold Palmer was top dog.

I was broadcasting a Pirates' game once. Ron Stone from the Phillies...have you seen the cartoons where the cat is chasing the dog and he hits the wall and he just slides down? Ron Stone was coming into second base to take Maz out, coming in high. Ron hit Maz and that goddamn strong leg. Slid down almost like slow motion. Slid right down and he was out.

Check the records in '66. The Pirates set the National League record for double plays, with Maz and Alley. Gene Alley was probably the best shortstop in the league then. I was still broadcasting in Greensburg on the radio. Mazeroski and Alley, in the middle of August, playing on grass fields, had only six errors between them. I think Maz had two and Alley, four. I mean, you drop that many balls playing catch in your living room with somebody! It's amazing. Nobody ever

Ron Stone

turned a double play any quicker than Maz did. Joe Morgan was the closest to him – and Joe learned a lot from Maz. He went to a smaller glove.

I started doing Pirate broadcasts in '67. It was tough. You know, jocks moving into the booth facing that antipathy toward jocks from those who didn't play the game. They'd

Dugout interview: Roberto Clemente with Nellie King

watched the game. They had paid their dues broadcasting, but so had I. But I had done something that they didn't do: I had played the game! Three guys in the booth are like three people in a marriage. Not too good. Bob Prince and Jim Woods were together, and I was the young guy coming in, the jock. They called me the jock sniffer.

But Bob Prince always spoke well of Maz. He'd say, "There's nobody who does the things that Maz does with the glove, nobody who can turn the double play like he does." Bob Prince was right.

*"**H**ow I loved to have Mr. Hoover out there, Mr. Vacuum at second base."*

– Bob Purkey

12

Bob Purkey

Bob Purkey was a crafty sinkerballer who pitched thirteen seasons in the National League from 1954 to 1966: five with the Pirates, seven with the Reds, one with the Cardinals. Bob was a three-time All-Star; his 23 wins and 5 losses for Cincinnati in 1962 is one of the finer performances of the post-World War II era.

I was born and raised in Pittsburgh in the Mount Washington area. I played sandlot and high school baseball. I was scouted by the Pirates, and went down to one of their tryout camps in Florida in early 1948. They liked what they saw and signed me up to a minor league contract in Greenville, Alabama. I played in the Alabama State League in 1948. Ended up with nineteen wins and eight losses.

From there to the Three-I League in Davenport, next stop New Orleans, and '51 and '52 into the service. In '53, I went back to New Orleans, and then in spring '54 I came up with the Pirates. I played with them through '57, then the Reds, '58 through '64, went to the Cardinals in '65, and back to the Pirates in '66. So I played with Maz and against Maz.

When Maz came up, he was a sucker for a curveball – could not hit the breaking ball out over the plate. He was a fastball hitter, inside and high; Maz had a difficult time with the breaking ball.

As he progressed and became more confident, he learned to hit that ball out over the plate. He would hit that breaking ball. I think it detracted somewhat from his home run power, but he became a lot better hitter, more of a threat. Maz knew what he was doing at the plate.

When I was with the Reds, he watched me warming up and noticed me working on a new change-up...I didn't have a great one. Even though he knew that I had never thrown it to him before and it was a fairly new pitch to me, up came a situation in the game where something clicked in his mind and he said, "Here comes the change." And I accommodated him. Maz promptly hit it off the scoreboard in Pittsburgh.

I don't think there's been a better fielding second baseman, especially turning the double play, in the history of the game. We often said when Maz made the double play, it looked like he never touched the ball.

He looked like he had a ninety-degree stovepipe and the shortstop would throw it into the stovepipe and then it'd come out the other side, just turn the corner. Maz had legs like two-by-fours. Or maybe four-by-fours. He'd never give up any ground at second base. Guys would slide into his legs and bounce off.

His glove looked like a pancake. No padding, no nothing. When he made the double play, the ball would hit his glove – he didn't catch it – and go into his hand, just bouncing off the glove. He never caught the ball unless he had to, to get the out at second base.

He was just a good guy to be around. In his quiet way, he was a leader on the Pirates. He complemented Willie Stargell, though he'll deny it. He would go out there and play the game, wouldn't bitch, wouldn't complain about anything. He enjoyed playing the game. He was a quiet, fierce competitor.

He knew if you hit it to him, you were out. His records prove that. As heavy legs as he had, he would move very well, especially to his left, and he got a lot of balls in the hole that some second basemen would not try for, much less get to.

I first met Maz when I was with the Pirates when he came up in '56. We just hit it off, got along well. I like to consider myself like Maz, a competitor. I didn't have overpowering stuff; I didn't have great stuff. I went out there and made it work.

Just like Maz. He didn't have the great batting ability. Sure, he could hit the home run. He was big enough and strong enough, but he had a glaring weakness on the outside part of the plate. He worked and worked at it, eliminated that weakness and became a better hitter.

*   *   *   *   *

I liked to pitch in Crosley Field. Our ball club was geared to scoring runs and hitting home runs. Wally Post, Frank Robinson, Vada Pinson, Gus Bell...we had some guys with the Reds who could hit the long ball and our ballpark was conducive to them. I was a sinkerballer, and I figured as long as I make batters hit the ball on the ground, they can't hit it out. I didn't mind pitching in the small ballpark. It was a distinct mental advantage. When the opposition would come in, pitchers would draw straws and whoever got the short straw had to pitch there.

Maz and I were good friends and when he asked me to be his best man, I felt very happy, very privileged. But for some reason we were late getting back from Cincinnati so Maz put off his wedding until I could be there. We're still good friends. We still call on each other, help each other. He hasn't changed. Very unpretentious, down-to-earth. He doesn't forget his friends or his background. That's part of not becoming too big for your britches. He's got a lot of friends. A lot of people would do anything for him because of the kind of guy he is.

The '61 season with the Reds in the World Series? Everybody says we backed into it, but we won enough games to win the pennant, though we really died the last two weeks of the season. The Yankees beat us four games to one in the Series.

During the 1962 season, it was very difficult for me to believe what was happening. When I needed a run, I got it; when I needed an out, I got it; if I needed a great play...it was an unbelievable year for me. I had pitched well. I was 23-5, had a 2.81 E.R.A. But I wouldn't lose a game 1-0. I'd win it 2-1. I'll never forget it as long as I live...it was a thrill. I struggled to get the twentieth and the rest came right after.

Spring training, 1961, a pennant season for the Reds

What really bothered me was the spring of 1963. I had that 23-5, couldn't wait until spring training. Went down there and worked hard, started the first exhibition game, pitched three hitless innings. Two days later, in a routine spring workout, I pitched batting practice for our guys in the Philly game. Couldn't get loose, couldn't get loose, throwing half-speed, three-quarter speed; then I felt something pop back here. Tore my shoulder three times in the next three years and had to retire. Today I can't throw the length of my small office building.

That was a trying, disappointing time. Going so good, get to the peak, then the bottom falls out. In '66 – September, I guess – the Pirates let me go. I couldn't break a pane of glass.

When I tore my shoulder I started thinking about a second career; I thought about insurance. I liked the fact that I would be dealing with people. I got my state license, and the day after I retired, I was in the full-time insurance business. Been in it ever since.

You go from up here salary-wise, prestige-wise, everything that goes with the major league pitcher, to the next day down here with no income. But it's worked out. I've worked hard at it, put a lot of time in it. Being a pitcher helped. I wasn't afraid to make decisions. I had to make a decision in twenty seconds, get rid of a pitch in twenty seconds. You weigh all the data, come up with a pitch and have confidence, or you're not going to do well with it.

Same thing here. Self-discipline, which a major league pitcher must have, helped me a great deal.

Maz had self-discipline. Maz is someone you would want your son to model after and be like because he's a good guy.

Maz's upbringing was excellent. I met his Mom, you know, a lot of years ago. You've got to give his Mom credit, but he had to grow up early. I think his Dad passed away early in life, relatively speaking.

Maz just did what came naturally to him. You are a major leaguer on the field, off the field, wherever you're at, because you've got kids looking up at you, you're a role model. Maz didn't have to work at that.

As a pitcher, probably the most important thing was my

infield. Up the middle was extremely important. I wasn't a strikeout pitcher. I was a sinkerball pitcher, sinker/slider, tried to get the batter to hit the ball on the ground. How I loved to have Mr. Hoover out there, Mr. Vacuum, at second base.

And that double play combination, the teamwork between Maz and Dick Groat, Maz and Gene Alley. Made it easier for me!

The more balls hit on the ground, the more I liked it. I still hold the record for the most put-outs by a Pirate pitcher in a game. Bob Skinner was playing first base and I was pitching against the Cardinals, who had a lot of left-handed batters. I stopped a line drive for one put-out. There were five ground balls hit to Skinner that he tossed to me at first base, so I had six put-outs. Skinner also set a team record, for most assists in a game by a first baseman. Fielding was extremely important to me. I always was a pretty good fielder. Self-defense!

I made a living breaking bats. I got the ball on the fists of the right-handers. I threw to their belt buckle. I broke a lot of bats. I'd just run that ball in on the right-handers...a slider here, a sinker there. I could pitch to any kind of batter. Inside ball hitter, I'd throw sinkers off the plate inside.

If you let the batter take advantage of you at the plate, that's like him coming into your kitchen, opening your refrigerator, and taking a stack of steaks out for his dinner. I did what I had to do to win the game within the rules without hurting somebody. The brushback pitch was part of my repertoire. One year I led the National League in hit batsmen. You've got to remember I pitched to a lot of right-handed batters inside. And they would get hit, but not by brushback pitches.

I have used a brushback. That used to be a sign of respect by the pitcher for the batter. "Hey, you're hurting me so bad that I've just got to get you thinking a little bit." Today hitters get mad when they get brushed back.

I'm not talking about bean balls. If you were to throw at a guy's head, you wouldn't hit him. That batter has the ability, or he wouldn't be in the big leagues, to get out of the way of the ball. If I wanted to hit a batter, I could. I'm throwing at three inches on the inside of the plate and three inches off, or three inches on the outside and three inches off: I'm throwing at six-inch targets. You mean to tell me I couldn't hit that batter if I wanted to? I could hit him in the ass.

When I pitched, some batters would dive over the plate. Harvey Kuenn was one. Frank Robinson's hands were often in the strike zone. Frank was so tight to the plate that he got hit a lot. That was his choice, standing on the plate. If you pitch out over the plate, batters are going to kill you.

Pitching is not throwing a strike over the plate. It's not merely throwing a strike or throwing a ball. It's throwing a strike at a certain place, a certain kind of pitch at a certain time with a certain reason. You have the ability to do that, you can become a major league pitcher.

* * * * *

When I was traded to Cincinnati from Pittsburgh, I didn't mind going down there. Roy McMillan at short, Johnny Temple at second, and the Reds had tied the National League record for the most home runs hit by a team, in 1956. I went down there in 1958 and was 17-11. I was traded from a last-place Pirate team – "Rickey's Rinky-Dinks" – to a club that might win the pennant, except they needed pitching. I knew I was going to play. In '57 in Pittsburgh, we finished in last place. Bob Friend was our leading pitcher, 14-18. I was the second winningest pitcher, 11-14. [Pirates' GM] Joe Brown said at the end of the year, "We've got our pitching staff set for 1958. Friend, Kline, and Law."

"Where's Purkey?" That was a damn good question. Couple of weeks later, I find out I was traded. I was glad to go, because if they didn't have plans for me, the second winningest pitcher on the club, I wanted to go. It was the best move that ever happened to me in baseball, going with the Reds.

The Pirates said, "We're trading him to Cincinnati because we don't feel he can go nine innings." That year, I went 17-11. Completed seventeen games, more than any pitcher on the Pirate staff. We were expected to go nine innings every fourth day. Now they go six every fifth day.

Normally the day after a start I would not do any throwing at all. I would put on a rubber suit and try to work up a good sweat, get some aches and pains out. Second day after, throwing, either in the bullpen, light throwing to loosen muscles up again, or maybe even batting practice. Next day, light workout, and ready to go the fourth day out pitching. Just a matter of keeping your legs in shape, keeping your body in shape, throwing in the meantime.

I always slept with a shirt on, always wore a wool shirt when I was playing, even in summer, underneath my sweatshirt. I used to let the arm drain after I'd pitch. I would take a little strap with a hook on it, and I'd hook it up on my locker and just let my arm hang there, let it drain out naturally. That had a tendency to eliminate aches and pains.

I started the third game of the '61 Series and I got beat on Maris's home run, his 62nd of the season. I had them beat 2-1 going into the eighth inning. I completed that game, the first game of the Series at Cincinnati. Yogi Berra hit a pop fly into right field, and Frank Robinson came in to catch it; Elio Chacon runs into him and the ball drops. That led to the Yankees' first run. Then Blanchard pinch-hits a home run to tie the game up in the top of the eighth. Maris hit his home run in the top of the ninth to beat me 3-2. My most memorable game, if you want to call it memorable. I can't complain. I pitched a good game against them. But it could have been the other way so easily and we would have gone ahead two games to one. We were 1-1 going into that third game...that could have been the turning point of the World Series. The rest of the games, we got our jocks knocked off.

Mickey Mantle had that problem with his hip bone bleeding, but he played in my game, I know, because I struck him out twice. I had a good game going there. I can still see it.

I remember I pitched Opening Day for the Reds in Cincinnati. My first start as a Red against the Pirates. I beat them. Four days later, I pitched the home opener in Pittsburgh for the Reds against the Pirates again. I beat them again. Two Opening Days and I win both of them. Little things you remember.

I always went down to spring training five to ten pounds

underweight. Underweight. I figured the less body I had to get in shape, the easier it was going to be. I'd work out down there, running and conditioning the body more so than the arm. Without strong legs, you're in trouble. You start to do something strenuous when you're not in condition, the legs get rubbery. When your legs get rubbery as a pitcher, it means you're not in condition and you lose control. I was a control pitcher, so I couldn't afford that. I worked hard to stay in shape. I never wanted anybody to come up to me and say, "You lost that game today because you were not in shape." It never happened to me.

Favorite ballpark? Crosley Field. I liked to pitch in San Francisco too, because it was cold, the infield was soft, and I'd hit those Giants batters on the fist part of the bat and give them a handful of bees.

* * * * *

We're not talking about Maz; we're talking about me. Maz is good at whatever he wants to do. It's that simple. I don't care what it is. He's a good guy. That's all I can say. And I know that's not going to sell books.

Maz belongs in the Hall of Fame...I'm not sure it's going to happen. I'd love to see it happen because he deserves it. I'll be there to pull for him. I guarantee it. As long as I'm physically able.

*"**H**e is the type of friend that you would want in a foxhole with you. That's Mazzie."*

– Nellie Briles

13

Nellie Briles

Nellie Briles made the big leagues at age 21; he would soon pitch in the World Series. At age 24 he won Game 3 for the Cardinals in their epic triumph over the Red Sox in 1967. The next year he lost Game 2 to Mickey Lolich and the Tigers, and had a no-decision in the Cardinals' Game 5 loss (Detroit won the Series in seven games). Traded to the Pirates, Briles pitched the pivotal Game 5 of the 1971 Series won by Pittsburgh in seven games over Baltimore. Briles shut out the powerful Orioles on two singles. A ferocious competitor, Briles parlayed excellent control, and a willingness to let hitters put the ball in play, into a 14-year career with St. Louis, Pittsburgh, Kansas City, Texas, and Baltimore. A former Pirates broadcaster who is an accomplished public speaker, Nellie now handles corporate relations for the Pirates.

M az took such pride in his defense. Positioning, timing, game situations, little things that make up winning baseball. More than just catching the ball. His reputation is deserved as the finest at turning double plays in the history of the game. I have never seen anybody before or since Maz turn them as well. If you were to put him on second base today, I dare say Maz would turn the ball, getting rid of it, getting it to first base, better than anybody in the game today, 22 years after he retired! Defense is what he did best, yet he also led the Pirates in RBI's one year, hitting eighth, an incredible feat.

I only played with Maz for two years, '71 and '72. Until you see someone go about his daily business, watch how serious he is about the work that he does, his attitude, how he interacts with players, you never fully appreciate him. One day soon after I joined the Pirates, Maz was playing second base, left-handed pull hitter up, while I was on the mound checking a runner on second base, the tying run. Winning run at bat, two outs, ninth inning, I check the runner on second, and see Maz playing up the middle. Now we'd gone over these guys and with a left-handed pull hitter, a second baseman's supposed to be over in the hole. First baseman, guard the line, second baseman, play the hole, shortstop, cheat up the middle. I stepped off and said, "Hey, Mazzie!" I motioned for him to get over in the hole. Saw him take two or three steps over in the hole and that was fine. Took my stretch again, checked the runner, Maz is back up the middle! I stepped off, he trotted in and said, "Nellie, all I'm gonna tell ya is trust me." He went back to second base. Got my sign, checked the runner again, Maz was still up the middle! I fired a pitch and the left-handed pull hitter pulls the ball in the hole between first and second base. If Maz had been playing where we'd thought necessary, he would have made the play. Running in, backing up home plate, I'm swearing under my breath at Mazzie because he should have been there and caught it, and the game should have been over and now I'm behind home plate, I see the throw coming in from Clemente. Perfect throw, the catcher tags the runner out, we win the ballgame. Everybody's happy.

I'm upset. Not that we won, but because Maz put 100 more gray hairs in my head. I go in the clubhouse, Maz is sitting by my locker and he says, "Sit down. You think that's luck, that Clemente saved you, don't you?" I said, "I thought he'd saved you, not me." Maz said, "Clemente and I have been working this play for a long time. If there's a base hit up the middle to center field, can Al Oliver throw somebody out at home? Or if there's a sharply hit ball to right field to Clemente, can he throw the runner out at home? With a left-handed pull hitter, I'll play up the middle, I'll take away the ground-ball base hit or a possible line drive, gambling that if the ball is hit sharply enough on the ground or lined near Clemente, one of two things can happen. They'll hold the runner at third, or they'll send him and Clemente has an excellent shot at throwing him out at home plate. How did we make out?" Now I understood. I was in the presence of two great players, Clemente and Mazeroski, who were thinking of ways to help win ballgames.

* * * * *

Maz had a gift from God of absolutely magnificent hands. The coordination of his hands and eyes was very special. You could work all you want and never develop that kind of speed, dexterity that Maz has. He was given that gift and he polished it. When Maz turned the double play you'd swear he never even caught the ball. You'd swear he just ricocheted the ball all the way to first. But I never heard anybody complain that Maz was not in full possession of the ball. You compliment him.

If you don't have to catch it and you can somehow ricochet it with your hand and shoulder, everything all in the same motion, more power to you. People didn't realize how strong an arm Bill had. He developed that side-arm throw, worked on it hard. He used to talk to me about playing catch with his right elbow held tightly against his side, just practicing that quick flip with the wrist and developing that throw, not over the top, but that quick throw that he had to have to turn a fast double play and still get something on the throw. He had to practice and build up his arm to be able to do that. Things didn't just happen to Bill. He knew what he needed to do and did it. Maz took such great pride in his defensive skills, yet he was still a fine clutch hitter. You really had to be careful when you were pitching with men on because he would be a threat. He stung the ball, he had power.

I was born and raised in northern California. Born in a town that doesn't exist anymore, Dorris, on the Oregon border. It's a ghost town; there may be a gas station. Moved to Chico, in northern California, and played in all the leagues: Little League, Babe Ruth, American Legion and high school ball. Went to Santa Clara University down in the San Francisco Bay area and played semi-pro ball. After my sophomore year my father passed away; I went away to Canada, played semi-pro ball and then signed in September that year with St. Louis. I went immediately to the Instructional League in St. Petersburg, Florida; I'd signed a year before the draft was instituted so I could sign with anybody, and St. Louis seemed the best opportunity.

Played one year of Double A ball at Tulsa, and the next year, with the bonus rules then, if you got more than $8,000.00, you had to count against the major league roster for one year, or other teams could draft you. I was protected, as was a pitcher by the name of Steve Carlton. So we sat on the bench for a little while in 1965 and then I got to pitch quite a bit, Steve not as much until the second half of the season. Then after that, you have to make the club, which I did in spring training in 1966, while Carlton did not. They sent him to Triple A. Then in 1967, we were the world champions. I had played winter ball in 1966, after a tough season for me with St. Louis, 4-15. Just one of those things, anything unlucky would happen to you. The next year I went 14-5. Steve Carlton and I both went to winter ball in Puerto Rico and that probably helped us more than anything, because we got to play against pretty good competition. Take the ball and be in the starting rotation every fourth day.

The '67 Cardinals were well balanced defensively and won a World Championship; the next year we lost the Series. I was traded to the Pirates in '71 and we won a World Championship. I got to start Game Five of the '71 World Series and pitched the greatest game of my career. I pitched to

29 hitters; nobody got to second base. The two hits were dinky singles. I had tremendous command of my pitches. The next year, in the regular season, I came close to pitching a perfect game. I pitched to 28 batters. There was a questionable call on a ball hit by Ken Henderson to first base that Stargell couldn't pick up and they gave Ken the base hit. Henderson was the only guy who got on.

I went on to Kansas City, hurt my knee and really never contributed the way that I'd hoped. Texas, pretty much the same way. Then I went on to Baltimore in '77 and finished there in '78. I remember after I shut out Baltimore in Game 5 of the '71 Series, everybody was asking their manager, Earl Weaver, for quotes. When reporters asked, What about Nellie Briles?, Earl said, "I hate his guts, I hate his guts, I hate his guts!"

Six years later, in September, '77, Baltimore purchased my contract from the Texas Rangers. I hurried to Baltimore, where I started getting dressed around the 8th inning of a game, and sure enough when the inning was over, Earl came in the clubhouse, walked up to me and said, "You know what, I still hate your guts! I hate your guts, I hate your guts!" Earl chuckled, then went back out to the dugout.

*   *   *   *   *

One of the biggest lessons that I learned in the big leagues, what helped turn my career around, is throwing balls to be hit, instead of throwing pitches to be missed. But I wanted batters to hit the ball where I wanted them to hit it – when you have a middle infield like Maz and Gene Alley, let them hit the ball up the middle. That will cut down on the amount of pitches you have to throw. Your fielders will be on their toes constantly, ready to make the play.

In 1972 when Maz was substituting and a pretty speedy hitter topped the ball just past me, I knew it was a base hit because I thought Maz had been playing back, as there were two outs. There was a runner on third base and I tried for the ball and missed it; I just figured the runner would score. Suddenly Maz came in and made the bare hand play, that little quick flip that he had, and got enough on it to get the batter at

"When you have a middle infield like Maz and Gene Alley, let them hit the ball up the middle"

first. I just stood there amazed at this short squatty second baseman in the last year of his career. How in the world did he make that play? Later he said, "All I could think about is, man, if he tops it with a runner on third base, I won't get it, so I moved toward the infield, just a couple of steps." Intuitively looking at game situations gave Maz an edge.

Other special people in the infield? Brooks Robinson playing third base was magic. He was a Mazeroski playing third. Neither had a great arm, but they prepared themselves. The mental game. Always being in the game, knowing who's pitching, knowing what's happening, adjusting to pitches, to the type of stuff that a pitcher has on a particular night, that's what made them stand out. I don't know how you play short-stop better than Ozzie Smith. With his great range and the way that he can turn the double play, he can invent things when he has to.

* * * * *

Maz had a specific approach to the Forbes Field infield. You'd see opposing players go in there and they wouldn't take ground balls. No sir. Maz adjusted to the rock pile. The speed of the infield. The type of dirt. Maz was a leader. If you're to lead a team and inspire young people, you need to show them the professional way of preparing yourself to do your job and that's what Maz did. Always be on time, ready to play, take care of yourself. When you're taking your ground balls, you're just not taking ground balls, you're playing mental games, game situations, techniques, you're just not catching the ball and throwing it because you're supposed to go out there and catch ground balls.

Mazzie was the silent leader. Veterans and young players liked him. For a teammate, he had a great personality, friendly, approachable. He went about his business. He was friendly to the opposition to a point. But, when it came time to play the game, he was there to beat your brains out, day in and day out. He was there to compete.

Any time you'd see a great player like Maz, you would just pray that there would be some ball hit in the hole deep to the shortstop, who would feed Maz and he would turn it the way he could and just nick the fast runner at first and you'd say, that's impossible. He can't do that. Just like you'd want to see Clemente throw, watch Willie Mays run the bases. Or witness the sheer power of a Stargell.

My strong points? My biggest asset was control. I always threw the ball over the plate. I never had to worry. I could go out today and throw the ball over the plate, no problem. When I was a pitcher, I'd never pick up a ball, then go out and throw the ball over the plate. I could do that with almost all my pitches. Moving the ball around in the strike zone. Hitting the outside inch, the inside inch, throwing the ball up under the chin, when you need to without hitting anyone. Just missing off the corner outside. Moving the ball around, that's control. The other asset that I had was being competitive. I learned from Bob Gibson. There was a fire that burned inside of him; Bob was not willing to give an inch on his mound. I don't care if they've scored eight runs off of you, don't give up the ninth.

My first start was against Sandy Koufax in September, '65.

Sandy and I were hooked up 0-0 going into the bottom of the seventh. Two men out, Willie Davis reaches on an error, steals second; a little base hit, and they score a run. Sandy Koufax was intense through the first part of the ballgame. They score one run, a different demeanor. You could see it on his face: this game is mine, it's over. He walked to the mound in the eighth and ninth and nailed us, so I got beat 1-0. I lost, that's all I could think about.

The next day's batting practice, the Dodgers were finished and we were just going on the field, Sandy went out of his way to say, nice game, you know, too bad you had to lose. Don Drysdale with his wit came by and confided, "First major league tip. When you face a pitcher like Koufax, never give up the first run."

I never won twenty games, won nineteen, but the thing I'm most proud of as far as my career goes is that people considered me a winner. If it was a tough game, they wanted me on the mound. I think that's the biggest compliment a player could receive or want.

After baseball I went back to school, I went to seminars, Dale Carnegie courses. In college I took speech courses. I did stage plays. I did things to give me presence, confidence, and that has served me well since playing baseball. I was able to get into broadcasting working in Pittsburgh for Jones & Brown, Inc. While in St. Louis I started a business in electronics. I did not know anything about it. I learned how to set up accounts and call on people and develop relationships. When it came time for me to make the transition from baseball, to earn an honest living, I had choices. I'm comfortable calling on the corporate community. I'm in corporate relations for the Pirates, not so much ticket sales anymore, but out in public more, emceeing benefits, conducting baseball clinics for young people, running the Pirates Alumni Association.

* * * * *

Maz never looked at his job playing ball as work. He never looked at being a coach as work, which it is. It's a very professional job and perhaps he didn't realize the special skills that he had. He has fine communications skills. He taught Tim Wallach, who was a below-average fielding third baseman, how to properly catch the baseball, improving the position of his feet and his rear end and his approach to watching for the ball hit at him. And Maz helped Julio Cruz at Seattle become an outstanding defensive second baseman.

The Pirates Alumni Association fills a desire that Maz and other Pirates have to help other people and help teammates in trouble. It's a public charity; we raise all our own money and give it all away. No employees, everybody's volunteer. Except some legal expenses. Support from the ball club makes it go too. We've set up a special assistance program that's all confidential, with a 1-800 number guys can call to receive help. We've got wonderful stories people don't know about; it's the willingness of folks like Maz to be involved that creates that opportunity to help.

* * * * *

But you know, Maz and I did get cited once for catching too many trout in Pennsylvania. We didn't know the limit dropped from 6 to 3 after October 1. We had to appear in front of the fish commissioner; this big, burly guy behind a desk starts raising Cain with us. "Who do you think you guys are? You can catch all the fish you want, you think you own the world, the law doesn't apply to you? I ought to take your fishing pole! I ought to take your car, I can, you know, I can!" The guy's name was Tom Qualters. He said, I don't know how to add, so a hundred dollars a fish. I said, man, you've got to be kidding me. Then Tom and Mazzie start breaking up. Tom Qualters used to pitch for the Phillies and White Sox. Maz knew him and they were puttin' on the dog for me. We ended up being fined twenty bucks each.

Maz can make fun of himself too. Once he bought a wine-making kit, went down to the produce yards and bought grapes, experimented, and made 200 gallons of good wine. Maz decided if some Italians call their strong homemade wine "Dago Red," he would just call his, "Polack Purple."

* * * * *

Mazzie told me the greatest play that he ever made was with the tying run on second base, the runner running, and a ball hit way in the hole between first and second base at Forbes Field. Maz ended up running, trying to chase down the ground ball way in the outfield grass. All his momentum was carrying him toward the outfield, so the Mets were trying to score the runner. Tommie Agee was the fast runner from second base and Maz said, it had to be instinct, but I caught the ball in the tip of my glove and reached in while I was still running, turned around, and threw, not trying to pick up where home plate was, but just instinctly knowing. Maz threw Agee out at home plate. Perfect throw, out at home. So it's ironic, the greatest single play Maz ever made wasn't a double play!

Maz did amazing things on that Forbes Field infield. It would be interesting if any of the current players could go back in time and try to take ground balls on that Forbes Field infield. I wouldn't. You would take ground balls side saddle, you weren't going to face them head on, even with a protective cup.

* * * * *

Maz never wanted to toot his own horn, never thought of himself in too high or too low a light. He demanded your respect without trying to, just by the way he acted. Maz was the consummate professional, which is the highest compliment I can pay somebody. He is the type of friend that you would want in a foxhole with you. That's Mazzie.

*"**I** learned from Maz not to make excuses."*

– Steve Blass

14

Steve Blass

Employing a herky-jerky motion that he likens to "a barnful of owls coming at you," Steve Blass pitched ten seasons for the Pittsburgh Pirates, compiling a 103-76 record. Blass led the National League in winning percentage during 1968, "The Year of the Pitcher," with a sparkling 18-6 (.750) mark. Steve also led the league with five shutouts in 1971. That year in the World Series, Blass beat the Orioles 5-1 on three hits in Game 3, and 2-1 on four hits in Game 7. Both victories were complete games, and Blass's E.R.A. against Baltimore's sluggers was a microscopic 1.00. In 1972, Blass was a National League All-Star; two years later, at age 32, he would be out of baseball. His control of his pitches had mysteriously vanished; experts could not explain why. Steve became a Pirates' broadcaster in 1986, and today enjoys a well-earned popularity describing a game he played well.

I was born in Canaan, Connecticut in 1942, so I was eight years old in 1950, close to when Little League baseball started. The neighboring town was big enough to have a Little League, and I was driven there. My Dad managed, so I was assured of getting some playing time. I hid his keys one time until he promised me that I could pitch. I played mostly third base. Led the league in home runs with two. My father was a semi-pro player in the Sunday league; we'd have catches and play.

This year, he came to visit in Montreal; he's seventy-four years old now. He said, "I'm getting along now and the one thing I'd like to do that we haven't done in forty years is have a catch." So we had a catch at Three Rivers Stadium during the All-Star break, which was kind of neat.

I had a very strong arm and always threw the ball real hard. I tried a curveball and found I could make the ball bend. I was fascinated with tricking batters instead of overpowering them. You realize, "Boy, I can not only get them out; I can make them look bad." And that's fun. It's also a trap – you forget about your fastball. That happens all the way up to the major league level.

Our field was on a hillside in grammar school; if you made a single, you were assured of scoring because the rest of the field was downhill. But it was tough getting to first base.

Playing high school ball in Connecticut is unique. You schedule thirty games and play about twelve because of the weather. But we had a very good program for a small high school in New England. We had nine pitchers sign pro contracts in twelve years.

Three of us made it to the big leagues: myself and Tom Parsons, my wife's cousin, and John Lamb, my wife's brother.

We were given a handbook when we were freshmen. Housatonic Valley Regional High School baseball fundamentals. How to play the game. It was not to be taken lightly. I pitched three no-hitters my junior year, and two my senior year; Ed Kirby, my coach, prepared me well to go into professional baseball. It's a difficult transition.

Ed said, "Take a look at the field before you play. See if it's been raining or it's soft or the grass is high or which way the wind is blowing. Take five minutes and you can save yourself a lot of grief and give yourself a little advantage by checking out conditions."

Ed Kirby had a loose affiliation as a bird dog scout with the Pirates. I was courted by a lot of major league teams and scouted a good bit. In 1960, the Cleveland Indians said, "We'd like to sign you. We'll give you twenty-five hundred bucks as a bonus, then come to spring training the next year." I wanted to play right away. The Pirates came along and offered me four thousand dollars, plus I could play right away.

So I flew to Pittsburgh with my Dad and my high school coach and the Pirate scout, Bob Whelan, one of the most impressive guys I ever met.

I had never flown. We took off and the plane banked just a little left. I thought we were going to tip over. I got up and tried to go over to the other side of the plane to balance it. I was scared to death.

We got to Pittsburgh and I threw in the bullpen, with no idea how I was being evaluated. The Pirates signed me and I went to Kingsport, Tennessee, to the Rookie League.

My second night in Kingsport, Tennessee, I had this money – I had never had money in my life – and I went out and bought a six-pack of beer and a watermelon, and never left the room for about three days, it seemed like. I thought, I can buy anything I want. I got quite sick; maybe I learned something. I would mail my laundry in a box with a strap around it from Kingsport back to Falls Village, Connecticut. My mother would do it and mail it back.

Then Class D, Dubuque. I didn't do very well there. 1960 was the summer that the movie, *Psycho* came out, and we were in Keokuk, Iowa. I went to see it, then barricaded myself in my little hotel room, a sleazy room that looked like one from the Bates Motel. I was terrified. That's what I remember about that summer.

I went to spring training in 1961, feeling pretty good that I had signed with the world champions. Fort Myers, Florida was where they had spring training. The Pirate clubhouse at Terry Park had major league guys in one section, and a back room for minor league invitees. We didn't go in that main room. We'd look around the corner and say, "Oh, there's Maz," or "There's Face" or see Law or Friend or Groat and it was a great experience. I had not yet turned nineteen.

In 1961 I went to a Class D team in Batavia, New York, and had a very good year. Gene Baker was the manager, the first black manager for a major league organization at any level. Gene was a good pro, patiently encouraging us young players.

I pitched in the Arizona Instructional League against a higher grade of competition in the fall of '61 and in the fall of '62 against good prospects. Then in '62, I started the year at Asheville, North Carolina, A ball, got knocked around and sent back to B ball in Kinston, North Carolina. That was tough. I had never experienced much failure in baseball.

I was 17-3 in Kinston in Class B and had maybe my best minor league year. Every young player who is not a star-studded prospect – and I certainly wasn't – has to have a break-through year to get attention. The next year, 1963, I went to Triple A. That's a big jump, B to Triple A.

I did okay in Triple A. At the end of '63, I went to pitch in the Dominican Republic. Got married at the end of the year.

Two days later, Karen and I were in the Dominican Republic, two years after Trujillo had been assassinated. Military people, machine guns everywhere. After one difficult series, the fans tipped over our team bus. I worked on a slider down there, the pitch that got me to the big leagues and gave me seventy-five percent of my success.

I got off to a good start in Columbus in 1964, and the Pirates brought me up; I had one relief appearance against Milwaukee, then I got my first start in Dodger Stadium against Don Drysdale.

But we changed managers at the end of '64. Harry Walker came in, and sent me back to Columbus. We won the International League in 1965; I came up in 1966 to the big leagues to stay.

* * * * *

I was always very impressed with Bill Mazeroski because I thought he was a good pro. He didn't say a lot. I wondered constantly what he was thinking about me. Does he know who I am? Does he know my name? When I think of Maz and early impressions, I was trying to gain his approval, because he was the pro. No flash and dash, but coming from a conservative New England background, I'm more impressed with a person who does rather than says.

Maz never made any excuses; that's probably one of the best things I ever learned from him. He had that philosophy. People don't care why you didn't; they don't want excuses. You either do or you don't. Don't need to have a lot of dialogue about it.

The best thing that happened in my relationship with Maz was after the World Series in '71, when we won the seventh game, 2-1. Maz came up to me and said, "You're a real pitcher now. A lot of guys can pitch behind. I want to see how pitchers do when they've got a skinny little lead like 1-0 or 2-1. Anybody can pitch behind, but today you pitched ahead when it was on the line. You weren't behind 2-0 and all of a sudden we scored and then, boom, you got the win. You had to protect the lead." That was effusive praise from Bill Mazeroski.

You'd get conditioned to Maz making the double play. People used to accuse me of walking people on purpose to watch him and Alley turn a double play. The double plays all run together. Always so good. What I remember most about him making double plays is guys that would come in and try to break it up. I saw Bill Buckner carried off and I saw Ron Stone carried off.

Maz got to second base, planted himself, and created his angle with his legs. He always said his feet were as important in turning the double play quickly as his hands. Maz would get over there and the angle would already be established. I have this vision of him standing with his feet on both sides of the base getting the ball at the same time the runner would try to come in and crumple that left leg. Stone tried to take him out high and just kind of melted down the side of Maz's left leg.

* * * * *

Fielding was important to me. I had good reactions but I didn't fall into the trap of putting my fielding before my pitching. I had a very awkward motion, like a barnyard door opening and closing. I would fly all over the place. I would wind up with my back toward home plate following through toward first base; I got hit all over the place.

Nothing is more important than the pitch. A lot of balls would get hit up the middle in back of me. But I thought I was a little bit better than average fielder. And my herky-jerky motion made it hard for batters to pick up my release point.

I also had a very good pick-off move to first base, a very quick move. The throw to second I would seldom try.

I'd spin around and not throw, just to show I was paying attention. But I got a lot of pick-offs at first base. I was quick and I would cheat a little bit. I would come to a set position and throw before I turned, then turn and make a couple of steps to convince the umpire that my movement was to first base. It was always a balk, but I would get away with it. The runner was deceived because I'd be throwing the ball before I'd turn, while I was still in a set position. My body is still lined up to home plate, but I'm throwing – and then moving – to give the illusion that it's all part of the same movement. Just a half-second after release, I would make my body go toward first base to sell the umpire on the idea of one movement.

It was cheating, but not as much as left-handers do, throwing to first base. Left-handers should have to buy a ticket to come in the ballpark, they get away with so much.

When I came up and stuck, it was a transition period because Friend and Law were winding down; ElRoy Face would leave in 1968. I learned a lot from Bob Friend, my first roommate, about pitching and how to handle myself in the big leagues. Vernon Law was a great example. Harvey Haddix. ElRoy Face was great to be around. I learned a lot from Jim Bunning. Jim was 4-14 for the Pirates when they expected a lot from him, but he also could have been 4-6, maybe; he kept pitching when he was hurt.

I learned from Maz not to make excuses. I learned from Bunning that sometimes you've got to go out there when you're not one hundred percent.

"My herky-jerky motion made it hard for batters to pick up my release point"

When I was having trouble in a game and the manager was trying to buy some time to get a pitcher ready in the bullpen, every once in a while he'd tell Maz to come over and talk to me. I don't think Maz was comfortable with that. He'd come over, almost apologetic, "Well, they wanted me to come over here and talk to you." And I'd start feeling worse for him than I did for myself. He was so uncomfortable – I'd start forgetting that I was the one getting my head knocked in! I'd say, "I know what you're doing, Maz. Don't feel bad. I know you've got to do this."

Dock Ellis came up in the late '60s, a brash young man full of confidence. I got along well with Dock. A lot of people didn't take time to get to know him. Once he came out with curlers in his hair at Wrigley Field and we're all sitting on the bench in the bullpen. Sometimes day games in Wrigley Field present a little problem from the night before, so we're trying to get some sun and get our act together. Dock comes out with the curlers and you talk about guys flying. Nobody wanted in the picture. We didn't resent Dock for doing that; that was Dock, and he did that kind of stuff. But we didn't care to be in the picture with him, because there were fifty photographers trailing him looking for pink hair curlers. Dock did his own thing.

My favorite pitcher was Juan Marichal. I thought he was the cat's meow. Five pitches thrown from five different angles, essentially twenty-five different pitches! Marichal was a complete pitcher who could throw a lot of different pitches anywhere he wanted to. Great pitching sense.

Tom Seaver was one of the most overpowering pitchers. Guys that overpower you usually throw the ball down the middle and succeed. Tom was overpowering to spots.

Koufax had two dominant, overpowering pitches, a power fastball and a power curve. Gibson and Drysdale were mean guys who wouldn't give you an inch, who would knock down grandma if she crowded the plate.

I beat Don Drysdale in my first start, in Los Angeles. I remember approaching him, "Does the date May 13th, 1964, mean anything to you?" Don said, "No, why?" I said, "Well, I won my first big league game–" and Don said, "Not another one." That was a real date of distinction when you beat Don Drysdale for your first win!

My first home run? My only home run. I remember everything about it. Humidity, time of day, temperature. It happened to be on Mazeroski's 33rd birthday.

September 5th, 1969. Maz and I celebrated in Chicago rather well. We beat the Cubs 9-2. I pitched a four-hitter. Billy Williams got all four hits. First time since 1903 that somebody had pitched a four-hitter and one guy got all the hits. Two doubles and two home runs. I had four pitches; Billy got four hits off four different kinds of pitches.

I went 4 for 5 that day, my best day ever, and hit the home run in the first inning off Kenny Holtzman. Maz's birthday was a great day for both of us at Wrigley Field.

Willie Stargell was dominant in that ballpark. The Cubs had a reliever named Ted Abernathy, a submarine ball pitcher; it was almost cruel what Willie would do to Ted Abernathy. I always enjoyed starting in Wrigley Field. Stay in the ballgame long enough to get their pitcher out and get Abernathy in, then watch Stargell do something to get me and the Pirates a win.

You can always tell which way the wind is blowing at Wrigley Field by what the visiting pitchers do when their team bus arrives. If the wind is blowing in, they all want to get off and pitch; if it's blowing out, they want to stay on the bus.

* * * * *

I would like to see some of these guys who are setting fielding records play on Forbes Field, that rock pile. We would go away for two-week road trips and they would cover it with a tarp and bake it, so not only is it a rough surface, now it's hard. It's unfortunate that some of the records that are being set now are set on carpets. There's no bad bounce. I have a lot more respect for what Maz did than some of these sterilized records.

I hate the designated hitter. I didn't like expansion and divisional play. I think the game has been diluted. I temper that by noting that today's announcers make more money than past announcers. So I don't want to be too critical of the game.

I keep hearing about young pitchers coming up – great change-up, great off-speed stuff. You used to hear that he's got a great arm and we'll teach him other stuff. Where are those good live strong arms? These kids are eating better; they're conditioned better; they're bigger; they're stronger. How come they aren't throwing hard anymore? A guy is six foot six and his dominant pitch is a change-up? There are mysteries out there. Setting up off-speed stuff with the fastball is the opposite of the way it used to be.

* * * * *

Maz is kind of a contained guy. I thought he was the ultimate pro. He never made excuses. It's what you do, not why you didn't. And you don't have to blow your own horn. But I also saw a personal side of Maz. I roomed with him for half a year, maybe a year. He was hurt and couldn't play, and that really bothered him. He felt he should not have been on a major league ball club unless he could play. He was heading toward the end of his career, and Bill would not tolerate being embarrassed on a baseball field. You don't show anybody else up and you don't want to be embarrassed yourself.

I didn't appear in the '70 playoffs. I didn't have a real great year. Cincinnati beat us three in a row. With a good mix of good young hitters, and stabilizers like Mazeroski and Clemente and Stargell, we had a dynamite year in 1971, and won the World Series.

In 1971 our pitching staff featured Bob Miller, Bob Veale, Bob Johnson, and Bob Moose. Bob Newhart was not in the rotation that year, but he might appreciate the previous year's staff, which featured Moose, Veale, and Lamb. But in 1971 we became better pitchers because we were backed up by offensive support. You pitch with confidence, knowing you don't have to pitch 2-0 shutouts.

I had struck a lot of people out in the '71 playoffs, but I got knocked around; I tried to be a power pitcher, which I wasn't. So, approaching the World Series, I said, "I've got to be a slider pitcher, a control pitcher and I can't strike people out all the time." It worked out well. I had a three-hitter in the third game, and a four-hitter in the seventh game.

Bob Moose started the sixth game, and Murtaugh told me, "If this doesn't work out today, you're going to start tomorrow." There was nobody rooting harder for Bob Moose than I was, because I had had my moment in the sun in Game Three, and I said, "Go ahead and win it, Bob, everybody will be happy." I got the Game 7 opportunity. But I would have been fine if Bob Moose had won Game 6.

Clemente had a spectacular Series. Offensively and defensively. Roberto made a great throw to third base and the guy was safe, but we who saw it still remember it. And a one-hop throw to home plate when a guy should have scored from second base on a base hit – Roberto threw it from the warning track and I think it was Belanger who just stayed at third base. Never any intention of rounding third and scoring. Maz had a secondary role in that Series but he felt good about the outcome. Maz played on two World Series winners.

In 1972 I probably was more consistent than in any other year. I won nineteen games and lost eight. We went to postseason again. We lost the last game to the Reds abruptly. I pitched in that ballgame. I was ahead 3-2 when I left, Hernandez came in, then Giusti and Moose, and it got away and we wound up losing on a wild pitch. You're still tied, then wild pitch, it's over. You just sit there numb. The season is over. Everything you've done all year since February 15th. You think, "We've got to go in the clubhouse. We can't wear these uniforms for the rest of the winter."

Our manager, Bill Virdon, was very professional and acknowledged everyone's contributions. Clemente did the same, going around to different lockers and talking about having pride in what we had accomplished during the season. We learned there is no guarantee that just because you had a great regular season you're going to go to the World Series. One pitch and we didn't go.

That was Roberto Clemente's last game.

A couple of months later at a New Year's party in my house with Dave Giusti, his wife and some other neighbors, we got a call from Bill Guilfoile, the Pirates public relations man, about 4:00am, the first report of Roberto's plane crash. Roberto's death was a shock, as it would have been with any teammate. Above all it was a loss of a father and a husband for the Clementes.

In 1973 I had a very good spring training, and I was 3-3 at one point. I did not realize I was having trouble with control. Then it just started sliding away and I never got it back. Support was terrific from Joe Brown on down to teammates and people in the city. I don't think I got one negative letter.

It's tough when you're not contributing. I used to be the life of the party in the clubhouse – because I was helping. That has to come first. Who the hell wants to hear from the life of the party who's not pulling his share?

Twenty-one years later, I still don't know what caused it, why it happened. I tried everything I could, so in subsequent years, I'd have no qualms. I sleep very well.

I accomplished everything I wanted to; there's no tragedy in the story. I pitched in the World Series, an All-Star game, had a chance to be teammates with guys like Maz and Stargell and Clemente. Hell, I did everything I dreamed about doing.

I had a job three weeks after the Pirates and I parted company, working for Josten's, a high school class ring company. Spent eight years with them, and then worked for an Anheuser-Busch distributor before I got into announcing.

I'd always enjoyed being interviewed, going on radio shows. I felt very comfortable talking. I enjoy it, and I hope they never catch on to me. My idea is to project comfort, not get in the way of the ballgame, and relate well to the people I work with. You don't want to see or hear dueling announcers. Make it smooth, let people enjoy the ballgame.

I think Bill Mazeroski should be in the Hall of Fame. God bless Reese and Rizzuto, but don't leave Maz out.

Bill Mazeroski was the best second baseman that I ever saw. He was very consistent, he made the double play better than anybody, and he was a pro who played hard. Maz didn't talk a lot about his skills; he let you see them. No one compares to Bill Mazeroski as a second baseman. The other names fade away. I'm happy I had a chance to be a teammate of Bill Mazeroski's for some nine years. It was a delight.

"Maz gave you an honest day's work for an honest day's pay."

– Dave Giusti

15

Dave Giusti

A baseball star at Syracuse, Dave Giusti played basketball there with another two-sport performer, Heisman Trophy winner Ernie Davis. One of the original Houston Colt .45's in 1962, Dave was primarily a starter for four years before moving on to St. Louis, then Pittsburgh. Giusti led all National League relievers with 30 saves in 1971, going on to save all three Pirate wins against San Francisco in the divisional playoffs, as well as Game 4 of the World Series against Baltimore. A feared closer, Giusti was at or near the top of the National League in saves from 1970 to 1975. A National League All-Star in 1973, Giusti's palm ball baffled National League batters, who hit .219 against him at his peak in 1972. After seven stalwart seasons in the Pirates bullpen, Dave split his 14th and final season with the Oakland A's and Chicago Cubs. Dave is now involved in Pittsburgh area businesses.

I was born in Seneca Falls, New York, 30 miles from Syracuse. I played college ball at Syracuse University, basketball and baseball. I was signed by the Houston Colt .45's in 1961 and played about a half a year with the organization. In 1962, the first year the Colt 45's were a major league team, I began with them. I was a little bit over my head, and about August, I was sent down and tested, had a problem with my elbow and had elbow surgery that year. Too many palm balls at an early age may have been the problem.

I was sent down to Oklahoma City, the Triple A affiliate, in 1962, played until the end of the season, then played '63 and '64 for the most part in Oklahoma City. In 1965 the Astrodome was built and I became one of Houston's starters. Got off to a real great start, 6-0 before May 1, felt I was on my way. Reality set in, I ended up 8-7. I needed more seasoning. Spent the next few years with Houston and got traded, as a starting pitcher, to St. Louis. I started off well but then had some back problems and was demoted to the bullpen. I was in limbo at that stage of my career. The Cardinals traded me to the Pirates in the winter of '70. Trying too hard with the Pirates in spring training, I got off to a bad start, and they demoted me to the bullpen. Put me in long relief for a couple of weeks. Then they needed a short man, so I came in and did very well and that was the start of my career in short relief.

My awareness of Maz, if I may jump into that, began around 1966. I was with the Astros. Pittsburgh was winning 8-7, bottom of the 9th, one out and the bases loaded, and our catcher, Ronnie Brand, was the hitter. Ronnie had good speed for a catcher. The infield was midway, not back, not in, when Brand hit a ground ball in the hole that Gene Alley got and everybody on our bench thought, we're going to score the tying run, because you can't make the play at the plate.

Gene Alley caught the ball, and everybody thought there was going to be a force at second base, with a run scoring, leaving men on first and third, two outs. Alley threw to Maz and Maz turned that double play, just nipped Brand at first base and everybody was in awe. How quickly the ball got out of his glove, how quickly it got to first base, bang-bang play, double play, game's over. I had never seen anything like that. Players just stood there and said, How in the hell did that happen? That is when I first looked at Maz as a great second baseman.

I didn't notice how stable he was at second on the pivot, not jumping around, until I played with the Pirates and saw him play more. I will never forget one guy who played with the Philadelphia Phillies, Ron Stone, who went about 6 foot 2, 210. Running from first, he was coming in to interfere with Maz throwing the ball to first base. Stone comes in sliding hard and with his body tries to knock Maz down. Maz just stood his ground and Ron hit him high, a little above the middle of the thigh and he rolled down Maz's thigh like he was putty. They had to take Ron off the field with bruised ribs. I can't remember when Maz would have to jump or move laterally in order to avoid a slide into him. He was highly respected, another reason why he made so many double plays: baserunners didn't want any part of him.

* * * * *

One year Maz was down at Dream Week, a Pirates fantasy camp in Bradenton, Florida; guys pay three thousand dollars to get into uniform and we ex-players coach them. The night before it started we had dinner and a few cocktails. Maz and Pirates manager Jim Leyland got into a discussion about second base. For four hours, there they were, Leyland trying to tell Maz how to play second base, Maz getting on Leyland, "What do you know about it?" They had everybody in hysterics. People didn't understand that part of Maz. A lot of folks figured he was introverted, a loner, but when Maz gets into a certain environment with people he likes, he lets it out and has a good time. Another part of Maz that people don't see is what a fierce competitor he is. We used to play a lot of golf. He made some of the damndest shots you ever saw. He'd be in the trees and all of a sudden the ball was ten feet from the hole. Like how in the hell did he do that?

Getting back to my career, when I started out in Houston we played in Colt Stadium. It was not fun. That's the only place in all of baseball where Ernie Banks refused to say it's a good day for two. In fact, Ernie was carried off the field one hot Sunday afternoon, suffering from dehydration! Houston finally decided to play all night games. The mosquitoes were dive bombers, kamikazis. So large. Encephalitis was prevalent down there, so you'd come to the ballpark and smell this awful smell, the spray. The small clubhouses were not air-conditioned.

It was awful playing down there. So hot. You'd go through two or three sweatshirts when you were pitching and lose eight or nine pounds.

The Astrodome ceiling was a concrete structure with maybe seven by seven foot pieces of glass to let sunlight in. Grass would not grow there; without enough light, it died quickly. Monsanto came out with Astroturf but then you couldn't see the flight of the ball because of the glare. So then Houston had to paint the top of the dome, the glass part, so the glare wouldn't come into play. In '65 I lost many a game because my outfielders couldn't find the ball! Fly ball to left center field, where the hell is it? In the outfield it was always hard to keep your eye focused on the ball, especially when you'd turn your head. Plus, the speakers were too low and guys would hit the ball off them. This was the brand new Eighth Wonder of the World. On the road, Colt .45 attire was a western outfit, complete with cowboy hat and cowboy boots. Rather horrifying; to see some of the players with these outfits was hysterical. You'd go to New York City with a cowboy outfit on. What's this, the circus? That didn't last long. But it was different.

Pitching in the Astrodome, my goal was to keep the ball in the ballpark. Let the Astroturf help you; the balls that you think are hit slowly will get to the infielders a lot quicker, with more of a chance of a double play.

The palm ball was taught to me by Ted Kleinhans, my college coach. He had taught Jim Konstanty the same pitch with the Phillies. One of the Whiz Kids back in 1950, Jim was M.V.P. that year when they won the pennant. Ted Kleinhans was up with the Yankees for a short period of time, played a little bit of major league ball; he's deceased. He taught me that pitch, which helped Syracuse get to the College World Series in 1961; we came in third or fourth. The palm ball took its toll – it's a tough pitch to throw on a regular basis for strikes. It affects your elbow, because instead of using your wrist a lot, you more or less have a locked wrist, so that the ball ends up without a lot of spin. It behaves like a knuckle ball. Throw it as hard as you want and it's going to be only 75 percent of the speed of the fastball; at the same arm speed it disrupts the timing of the hitter. Fastball, one speed, palm ball, same motion of delivery, different speed. The hitter's out in front without good timing. And it helped that at times I threw my fastball in the low 90's.

Most memorable game? I think the one game that got me feeling confident with Houston was in 1965 against the Cubs. I pitched nine innings of no-hit ball in relief.

The Pirates elected me as player rep for the club in 1970. They've got to respect you to make you the middle man there.

You're the guy who will tell the rest what's happening in the Major League Players Association, potential problems between labor and management. I was player rep for five or six years.

* * * * *

Forbes Field's infield was different. It certainly wasn't the best and it usually was very hard. But maybe they wanted it that way because so many good Pirate hitters hit so many ground balls up the middle. It's amazing, seasons like '66 and '67 with Gene Alley and Maz, the tiny number of errors they committed on that surface.

My fielding abilities were honed in spring training – you keep on going over these basic drills, covering first base, throwing to second base. I had a little problem because I fell off to the left a lot. So balls that were hit right over the middle, hit hard enough, I couldn't get back to them; Bob Gibson, same way.

I think I was a decent fielder – I always liked to play in the infield during batting practice just to get ground balls. I'd sneak on. I enjoyed having balls hit to me. I could not stand to be in the outfield and sit there for thirty minutes waiting for a ball to come out there.

1970: Dave Giusti gets the very last out at Forbes Field, and a handshake from Maz

Getting the man at third when you've got runners at first and second takes practice. That's one ritual you work on as a right-hander. Left-handed it's easier, you can throw while turning. A right-hander has to grab it, turn, then throw.

Often though, unless it's hit very close to you, the play is not at third. You're usually throwing to second or first; if the ball is hit towards the base line, you'd better get that guy at first.

Entering the game in relief you have to be aware of the situation. The hitter, the inning, what the strengths and weaknesses of the hitter are. But you also have to rely on what you do best. You can't second guess and throw a good fastball hitter something else when your best pitch is a fastball. You have to throw your best pitch against him. It has to be. Just be aware of where you're going to throw it. There are some cases where a good hitter is a dead fastball hitter; maybe then you can go with your second-best pitch.

Very few batters get hits on low and outside, hard fastballs. So, if you are able to put the ball in that area consistently, fast-ball or curveball, you're better off than throwing your best pitch down the middle. My philosophy was throw the ball into an area where he's least apt to hit it hard. I knew what I had to do. Guy on third base. What's the pitch that's going to keep the batter from getting that sacrifice fly or hitting the ball hard somewhere? Most people don't realize the thinking that goes on, that confrontation between the pitcher and that hitter.

*   *   *   *   *

Mazeroski was a great influence on the younger Pirates. He had instant respect. They would listen. Another thing, he was very approachable. You went up to him and he would sit down with you.

When I was with Houston and St. Louis facing Maz, he was not an easy out. Good fastball, high-ball hitter, no question. When he was on and hitting the ball the other way, he was really tough.

Maz also made other players look great. Gene Alley knew that Maz was going to catch the ball wherever he threw it. So Alley's confidence was very high the whole time he was play-ing there. Gene Alley was a great shortstop, tremendous, great arm. But I think that having Maz as his second baseman made him even better.

Any Pirate pitcher, when he'd throw to second base, with a decent throw, had a helluva chance of getting out of the inning because Maz was going to get that ball to first base for a double play. Knowing that you have first-class defensive players behind you makes you feel good as a pitcher. Builds your confidence.

*   *   *   *   *

When I started playing professionally, I didn't dream about being the best pitcher in the world. What I dreamed about was surviving the minor leagues. Do well there, go through the learning processes, get to the big leagues.

In 1969 with the Cardinals we had Vada Pinson, Lou Brock, Curt Flood in the outfield, Joe Torre, Tim McCarver, Shannon, Javier, Gibson, Briles and we didn't win it. That was my first recollection of really wanting to be in a World Series. The next year, 1970, with the Pirates, we won our division, then lost to Cincinnati in the playoffs. Won the Series in 1971, but we had a better ball club in '72.

We lost to Cincinnati in the playoffs in 1972. That was probably the most disappointing thing in my career, giving up the ninth-inning home run to Johnny Bench. It is sad that fans remember Bob Moose throwing a wild pitch that let the winning run score. Bob did one hell of a job, because there were men on first and second when he came in; he got two quick outs and now with men on first and third it just so happened that the ball got underneath the catcher's glove. Moose did a helluva job and got to be the goat with me.

Forbes Field

Life after baseball at first was very hard. The first job was a 2 1/2 year stint as a sales representative for a machinery and fabricating company. Then with American Express my job was to call on corporations to get them to use our Corporate Card for business expenses. It branched out to using our travel agency. I signed most of the major corporations here in Pittsburgh and I'm very proud of that. Some of my co-workers said they'd never seen anybody so intense, so competitive. Well, short relief is a constant competitive environment.

Starters pitch, give up a couple of runs, then settle down. You can't do that in relief. And there was always the feeling of letting the club down. You never get used to it. The Johnny Bench home run I will relive for the rest of my life. The only consolation is that was the highlight of Bench's career.

* * * * *

Three Rivers Stadium

What made Maz different? His total dedication to his position at second base. His focus. His ability to play that bag as well as anybody could play it. He had a couple of things going for him. As good a pair of hands as anyone who has played second base and fielded ground balls, plus the quickest hands making the double play. You had to see it. Because how can you describe how well someone is playing defensively? It's hard to do. You can say they made a diving catch. How do you describe that this guy makes the double play better than anybody else?

Maz epitomizes the kind of work ethic and dedication to a position that has somehow been lost in today's environment. There are players today who have the kind of ethic Maz had, highly dedicated, but there are fewer of them. Just with the number of games that he played hurt during the course of his career, Bill Mazeroski typifies players of his era who were totally dedicated to the game. Maz gave you an honest day's work for an honest day's pay.

*"**M**az would come over to the mound and say, 'Let's get this son of a so-and-so out. Make him hit it to me.'"*

– Bob Veale

16

Bob Veale

As a Birmingham teenager, Bob Veale took his mother's advice and turned down an offer to play basketball with the Harlem Globetrotters; Bob would play major league baseball like local legend Willie Mays. Veale pitched for the Pittsburgh Pirates from 1962 to 1972, and for the Boston Red Sox from 1972 to 1974. From 1964 to 1970, this workhorse of the Pirates staff averaged 35 starts a season. An All-Star in 1964 and 1965, the 6'6" Veale led the National League with 250 strikeouts in 1964; in 1965 he struck out 16 Phillies in nine innings, still a Pirates record. That year Veale achieved a mark of 9.34 strikeouts/game, surpassed then by only Herb Score, Jim Maloney, Sandy Koufax, and Sam McDowell. Bob's career 7.96 strikeouts/game trails only the marks of Koufax, McDowell, Nolan Ryan, Roger Clemens, and J.R. Richard. Batters hit an anemic .236 against Veale, which helps explain his 3.07 career E.R.A. and record of 120 wins and 95 losses. Bob has shared his pitching savvy over the years by coaching in the Braves and Yankees organizations, and he plans to resume coaching.

I was brought up around baseball in Birmingham. I worked at Rickwood Field in the concession stands for Eddie Glennon, the general manager for the Birmingham White Barons. Those days there were White and Black Barons. I worked for both. I was ball boy and bat boy for the Black Barons. Willie Mays played with the Black Barons – he was a pistol. Catching balls barehanded, throwing runners out at home plate, hitting balls over the scoreboard – he was devastating. But Willie's Dad, they called him Cat Mays, he was the best ballplayer there was.

I had the opportunity to pitch to the White Barons – when there wasn't anybody in the stands. I was eleven, twelve years old. Eddie Glennon tried to sign me when I was fourteen or fifteen; I wouldn't sign. I told him I was going to go to college and he tried to entice me every way he could to get me to sign and I wouldn't. So I would eventually sign with the Pirates when I left St. Benedict's in Kansas, now Benedictine College.

In the early '50s in Birmingham, we'd gather around the radio and listen to the Brooklyn Dodgers and the New York Giants. Don Newcombe, Joe Black, Dan Bankhead pitching. Black pitchers in the majors. I thought I could do that too.

After college the Pirates took me to Chicago; I impressed them throwing a little bit in the bullpen, they signed me, and we got it on from there. I met Maz at spring training but I didn't get a chance to appreciate being around him until I got up with the club. We'd call him "Mr. No Touch." I haven't seen anybody field as well as him since, or ever. He and I got along real well. We would fish and hunt together and he still owes me a Jeep!

About '65, '66, I went down to his house, we were going hunting. He had this little old raggedy Jeep that he said wouldn't run; it wouldn't move. I said, I can get it moved. Maz said you can't: pick it up, you can have it. I turned it over for him. I never did get the Jeep. I always kid him about that.

As a pitcher you wanted the ball to go to Maz. You'd try to tailor your pattern of pitches for Maz or Gene Alley, because you'd know you'd have two good gloves to back you. Maz was to second base what Brooks Robinson was to third. If you needed a couple of outs, you wanted the ball hit to Maz; if Maz had anything to do with it, the hitter was gone. Very seldom did he bobble or boot a ball. I had a lot of balls hit back through the middle, because of my velocity and because I was trying to pitch the ball in an area where it would be hit in Maz's direction. If you needed a double play, you wanted Maz to be involved. Whether the ball was hit to him or he was the pivot, you were surely going to get at least one out.

Bill was special. I have never seen an individual work so hard at such a young age to be what he was. If you have a love for something and you're hungry enough, determined enough, that's the way to go about it, diligently. You can fool some people but you can't fool yourself. Bill never tried to fool anybody. He knew what he wanted to do and he did it. He wasn't Mickey Mantle at the bat. But he would hit .260 year in and year out with some power and that's pretty good for a middle infielder. He was a very good hitter in late innings, too. Bill was kind of like a diamond in the rough, cultivated into a gem. His kind only comes around once in a while.

I worked on my fielding, but I knew if the ball got past me, Mazeroski was going to catch it, because he was quick. A little chubby, but quick. Cat-like. Maz had feline agility with canine stamina.

Single game, double-header, didn't make any difference. He never did complain about being tired. You want to be around someone who is going to give you a hundred percent regardless of how many games he's played. Regardless of wear and tear on his body, which takes its toll. Maz never complained about being hit.

* * * * *

I was a power pitcher and I was all over the place. You might get it inside two feet or outside. Wildness can be beneficial to the pitcher. My best pitches were my fastball and low curveball but most of the outs came on sliders. I came up with a pretty change-up and a pretty curveball later on. The fastball you've got to come up with as a kid. Nolan Ryan – he

Strikeout artist Bob Veale with manager Harry Walker

could hardly hit the side of a barn, but he stuck with it and it paid off. Just like the Dodgers stuck with Koufax for four or five years while he was learning how to pitch.

In the minors I threw hard too. Threw a no-hitter. I remember striking out sixteen, eighteen batters. You can't live off that the next year. That's the way I looked at it. You have to keep progressing. That was B ball and I jumped to Triple A the next year. I had signed a three-year contract to play Triple A; I was up and down to Columbus and I stayed with the Pirates in '62 and '63.

When I got up to the majors and put the uniform on, everything was done hard. I didn't have the coaching or tutoring that I should have had. It was just like a weed. A weed will take over if you leave it alone, take over the whole farm. But I had a great deal of help from veteran pitchers like Bobby Shantz and Vernon Law. Just watching Vernon helped me. I would talk to him whenever I would get a chance and kid him a lot. I was always a chipper-type person. The only stranger to me was the friend I hadn't met. Actually the only stranger was the hitter. I had to get him out one way or the other.

* * * * *

I enjoyed being on the Pirates team that won the 1971 World Series. When you accomplish something together, everyone enjoys it. The next year though, I was released. I went with Charleston, then joined the Boston Red Sox and finished up in their bullpen in 1974. Then I came home, stayed out a year and got a job as a minor league pitching instructor with the Atlanta Braves and I stayed there for ten years.

I really enjoyed working with those prospects. I tried to be honest. A fellow who looked like he was going to be labelled minor league all his life, I'd try to steer him to thinking about the other end of baseball. The administrative part. My philosophy was, if I can help, I'm going to try. I didn't want it on my conscience that I could've, should've, would've. I come from a family of fifteen kids and a certain sacrifice has always been a part of our life. Those who have never experienced that have missed out on an important portion of life. That's why I felt I should divulge baseball knowledge that I accumulated, to other guys coming up. You can see guys doing something wrong and instead of letting it hurt them down the road, you try to prevent that.

* * * * *

Everybody today is trying to make a buck. You have an idea when you see a guy come up with a big old container of cards; signing one or two cards is fine, but why sit there and sign twenty cards for one person? You want one, I'll sign one. I don't have all night to stay there. My life has to go on too. I'm not going to sit down and fatten a frog for a snake, you know what I mean? I always had time for anybody who wanted an autograph or wanted to chat, or came on the field and wanted a baseball, and we were charged for those things. Pittsburgh charged us. It didn't bother me. I enjoyed doing it for the fans.

We were talking about Maz. He was a quiet leader. The way Maz would go, that's how the team went. Maz very seldom had a bad day. He very seldom made a mistake. Four or five a year, that's all.

Nobody could touch him with the glove, then or now. Nobody had the quickness or the hands. He could see the ball; it looked like he knew where it would be heading, in his mind, before the ball got to the plate and that's something you can't teach. Maz would come over to the mound and say, "Let's get this son of a so-and-so out. Make him hit it to me." But Maz was just like a river; he ran quiet. Everything he did was quiet.

Clemente was the opposite of Bill. He would have fun in the clubhouse. Telling jokes, everybody would bust out laughing. I used to have to rub Roberto down every day before a ballgame unless I was pitching. Clemente would want me to rub him down even sometimes when I was pitching that day! I would do it about every day for five minutes. The trainer would say, come on Veale, he wants you in here. Clemente played so hard. When he was on that field there was always something exciting about to happen.

Pitchers I admired? I never tried to pattern myself after anybody else, but I liked to compete against Koufax, Drysdale, Gibson, Bob Bolin, Fergie Jenkins, guys like that. When they walked out there, you would have to push your game up a notch.

Donn Clendenon, our first baseman, was my roommate most of the time with the Pirates. We didn't do too much together. Donn was an astute-type person, studying law. I would talk with him about what he was doing and sometimes talk about a ballgame for a while, maybe go out and have a drink, not often because I wasn't making that kind of money. With nine sisters and five brothers it was kind of rough.

Donn was always the articulate one, a real student. I enjoyed the time we had – we were like the Odd Couple. I was just a country boy, liked to do garden work. He's not like me, grappling for words, gasping like a fish out of water. Being a lawyer, Donn can tell you two or three lies in the same breath. Donn's a good fellow.

* * * * *

Back in '85, while I was working with the Atlanta Braves, I was in Greensboro, North Carolina with the Hornets. Somebody broke into my house in Birmingham and stole my baseball mementos including my 1971 World Series ring; then they doused the walls with some chemical and burned the house down. We moved and got this place here. I did all the work myself. The floors, everything. I do the cooking, you might smell the smoke in there, I burned up something.

In 1993, I was invited to the Pirates' Fantasy Camp. There were about sixty guys down there. I just hit it off with everybody. I didn't want anyone to go home and say they didn't get any hits. I'd talk to them, sign autographs, go out to eat. We just had a wonderful time. Those sixty guys got together and donated money to replace my Series ring! I had no idea. It brought a little water to my eyes. Doing that for me was really a humanitarian thing to do.

I'm going to try to get more involved in B.A.T., the Baseball Assistance Team, because it really is a worthwhile thing. It even helps guys who played in the old Negro American Ball League. These guys like Pat Patterson, I talked to Piper Davis a few months ago, a fellow named Shepard who lost his leg, B.A.T. comes to their assistance with mega-bucks.

* * * * *

I think Bill Mazeroski belongs in the Hall of Fame. Since Bill played in Pittsburgh, not New York or Los Angeles, the media don't whoop it up as they would have if he had been in one of those cities. I hope that Maz gets in before he doesn't know what he's in there for, you know what I mean? And I hope that he can get in there and appreciate it. If anybody deserves being there on his own merits, it is my buddy Maz, a great player, and a fine man. He's the kind of man you'd want your son to be like.

*"**M**az was more help in my adjustment to the Pirates and to the major leagues than any other person."*

– Donn Clendenon

17

Donn Clendenon

Donn Clendenon came up with the Pirates at the end of '61 and played a bit in '62; from '63 through '68 Donn started at first base. Donn's best year was 1966, when he hit .299 with 28 home runs and 98 RBI's. A free swinger, his total of 163 strikeouts in 1968 remains a Pirates record. Clendenon began 1969 with the Expos before joining the Miracle Mets later that season. Donn was the *Sport* magazine M.V.P. of the 1969 World Series, homering in Games 2, 4, and 5 as the Mets shocked the Orioles by dispatching them in five games. After two more years with the Mets, Donn closed out his 11-year career with a season in St. Louis. Donn Clendenon is a lawyer living in Sioux Falls, South Dakota.

My stepdad, Nish Williams, was my early influence. He had played in the Negro Leagues with the Baltimore Elite Giants, where he was the second-string catcher; the young third-string catcher was Roy Campanella. My stepdad had a great part in teaching Roy how to play defense.

Nish loved baseball – the regular diet at my home in Atlanta. My real father passed away when I was three months old so I never knew him. Nish Williams preached baseball. I enjoyed playing football, basketball, and softball, but I had to play baseball to get my allowance! Athletics was a great part of my life – it kept me out of trouble. And I had to achieve academically, because my parents would not permit me not to. It worked out very well for me.

Jackie Robinson, "Sad Sam" Jones, Joe Black, and Roy Campanella all had a great influence, too. At that time they were touring with the Jackie Robinson All-Stars. As they came through the South, with its "separate but equal" facilities, they stayed in private homes; most stayed with my Dad. So, I got a chance to meet those guys and be their bat boy when they were in town.

I remember as a youngster I was afraid of the baseball, so my Dad built a pen, and as he'd catch, he would have "Sad Sam" Jones and some of the great old pitchers like Satchel Paige come down and pitch. My Dad would put me in the batter's box, without a bat.

I was nine or ten. All I had to do was watch the ball. "Sad Sam" Jones was particularly scary because he was drinking a little bit and would throw the ball about fifty, sixty miles an hour, and hit me with that big curve. I became a pretty good breaking-ball hitter because I could pick up the rotation on a ball earlier than my peers could.

When I graduated from Morehouse College, I considered playing a little pro football. But I had a knee injury my last year in college and football didn't work out. I do remember they were honoring Jackie Robinson in Atlanta, and I was the College Athlete of the Year on the same program. I sat with Branch Rickey, who was a very, very astute individual.

Branch had left the Dodgers and was advisor for the Pirates.

He invited me down to spring training. He said I didn't want to play pro football or basketball; I wanted to play baseball! Branch Rickey was the kind of guy you couldn't disagree with.

So I went to an open free agency camp down in Jacksonville. I was teaching school at the time, having graduated from college. I took a ten-day leave of absence, went down and worked out in different positions.

After ten days, I left and went home, because no one said anything to me. Every morning they would put your name on the bulletin board; if your name was not there, you knew you were going home. My name had not been on the bulletin board, so I left camp and returned to Atlanta. I looked up in my classroom one morning and there was Branch Rickey, Jr., with Joe Brown, the general manager of the Pirates. I signed a "lucrative" contract – five-hundred-dollar signing bonus – and started off in Jamestown, New York, Class D.

* * * * *

I rose through the Pirate organization, playing four or five years in the minor leagues. You had a good year in Class B, you moved to A and just kept working yourself up progressively, like grade school. I think it was great because as major leaguers we had playing experience – more so than some kids today learning how to play in higher classifications.

They moved me to the outfield because I had good speed. My Dad had stressed that it's best to play more than one position.

I went to Triple A, and we won the pennant for the first time in a number of years at Columbus. I went back to first base. So I played a little first base and outfield in the minor leagues before I went to the major leagues.

That's where I met Captain Maz. I was a young guy who thought of himself as level-headed, but I was immature in many ways. And I still had some doubts, was still in awe about major league baseball. I do remember Mazeroski coming to me when I first got there and giving me a welcome.

I remember playing a spring training game down at Fort Myers the year before. A guy hit a shot to center field, where I was substituting for Bill Virdon. The ball took off – a knuckle ball, over my head. I felt bad about it, though I did hold the guy to a double. I got to the bench and Don Hoak, a veteran, jumped in my face. "Listen, you SOB, you've got to catch that f-ing ball!" Scared me to death. Maz came over and said, "Hey, Donn, don't let that bother you; that's just Hoak's way," which helped to alleviate the situation.

Maz was a quiet leader, and I really loved that guy. He was very bright and he knew how to handle men. I've never known Maz to criticize anybody.

He would tell me, "You've got a lot of great abilities. I notice how you get away from pitches when they're throwing at you. You just move your head, whereas I have to go down. You have good eyes, good reflexes, good agility."

Maz was the key to our infield. I mean, this guy could turn a double play. He had those big Polack legs, and the ball would never stay in his glove over a fraction of a second. One motion, on to first base. And was he accurate!

Maz was so quick that sometimes when I got to first base and turned around, the ball was right there. I had to catch it or it'd kill me!

He never was in any controversy. Never thrown out of a game. Always supportive. He never ribbed the players. You learn to respect a man like that. He's been that way throughout his life.

I'd have to say Maz was the greatest fielding second baseman of all time. I didn't see Bobby Richardson and other American Leaguers play, but I have not seen anybody better than Maz.

I remember I would dive after a ball, miss it, and Maz was always there. He'd catch hard shots, too, using the worst glove in baseball. A little pancake. I couldn't even get my hand in it!

We turned a lot of double plays. I knew we were great when we doubled up Maury Wills and Willie Davis, and it wasn't even close.

I could come in and choke bunters off in bunt situations because I knew Maz could get to second or first base, if need be. That would force the opposition to make a very good bunt. Many fans consider great defense boring now, but astute baseball fans enjoy it.

* * * * *

We had a good-hitting ball club, too. Clubs would save their best pitchers for us. So, when we went to L.A., we knew we'd be getting Drysdale and Koufax. Marichal and Sanford would be waiting in Frisco.

In one series, I homered off Drysdale one game and Koufax the next. I remember it so vividly. Drysdale had me struck out on a slider that backed up down the middle of the plate. The umpire called it a ball. The next pitch I hit out. Drysdale was really PO'd.

I'd say Koufax was certainly one of the greatest, but don't forget Bob Gibson, Juan Marichal, or Jim Maloney. Every team had stoppers.

On the Pirates, Roberto Clemente was one of the better athletes you'd ever find. Great physique. Great arm. The only thing I didn't like: he would handcuff me. Guy hits a ball to right field, goes around first base too far. Roberto would pick it up and gun it behind him. Boy, that ball would eat me up on the short hop.

Maz was more help in my adjustment to the Pirates and to the major leagues than any other person. He didn't have to teach us how to play baseball, but he was always boosting our confidence in a unique way.

Roberto didn't talk much. He'd be complaining about being sick, then go 5 for 5. Meanwhile I'm healthy and 0 for 4.

We had great players. Offensively, I was overshadowed by Willie Stargell and Clemente. Defensively, Mazeroski was the kingpin and Gene Alley excelled. So I always felt third best.

I did lead the team most years in game-winning hits. Maz used to tell me, when the game is on the line, I want you to hit. That would boost my confidence.

He would always give constructive criticism. Most players who played with Maz felt they were impacted by him. He made everybody better.

I remember once on a great double play Gene or Maz went

all the way behind second base, caught the ball and flipped it over to the other, who turned and whipped the ball my way – I didn't know where the ball was. Here I'm trying to find first base and the ball at the same time!

It was easy to stretch on Maz's throws. You could judge how far you should stretch to get it. The ball wouldn't move on me. I would sense the runner and occasionally I'd cheat a little bit. I could stay on the base most of the time.

I didn't stretch as much on Gene's balls because if I get out there and that ball moves, I'm dead. Gene threw smoke, and his sidearm and overhand throws moved in different ways.

I didn't cheat as much as some first basemen do, because I had a good stretch. All the way out. I have long arms and long legs. I didn't need to drag my foot off the bag. Maz would work with me on my footwork, to help me get it comfortable.

I started off stealing bases. Then I jammed my wrist a couple of times, and Joe Brown told me, "Drive in the runs; let the other guys do the stealing." I could run. I had great speed for

"It was easy to stretch on Maz's throws"

a big guy – I once hit an inside-the-park home run against the Braves, and I hit 14 triples one year.

I worked every day I played major league baseball. Not too many people know that. I worked with corporations and industry. In Pittsburgh, I worked at U.S. Steel, Mellon Bank, and in the District Attorney's office. I'm an early riser. What are you going to do all day? Only so many movies to see.

I was playing ball with the Pirates when I started at Duquesne Law School. It got to the point where I was hitting .301, then .299 and .249, and I'm distracted because I've got to study. Joe Brown said, "Decide, make a choice. You're a law student or you're a professional baseball player." Hell, there wasn't any choice. I dropped out of school.

My father took ill and subsequently passed away; he was instrumental in my life and I had a hard time concentrating. So I did not resume my law studies until I had gotten out of baseball.

Negotiating contracts was interesting. I had a propensity for striking out, the first thing Joe Brown would mention – always my negatives. I'd go in there wanting a ten-thousand-dollar raise, and the next thing I know, eighteen hundred. So I started getting smart. Rick Roberts of *The Pittsburgh Courier* became my statistician.

Next time around, after I had a pretty good year, Joe Brown says, "Donn, you still struck out a lot. Not a hundred and thirty-six this time, but a hundred and twenty-eight times." And I replied, "Yes, Joe, but I led the team in game-winning hits. I had the highest batting average with men on second and third base." I just went down the list. Joe said, "How did you get all those stats?" I got my highest raise that year. You know who was grossly underpaid – Mazeroski, the premier second baseman in all of baseball.

Before the 1969 season, I quit baseball. I was making as much money out of baseball as I was in the game. I became Scripto's Vice President for labor relations and corporate relations, a job that involved union negotiations. I didn't have spring training that year. I decided to get back in, and started the season with the Expos, who had taken me in the expansion draft from the Pirates.

As soon as I started rounding myself into shape – hands, feet, timing, defensive timing as well as offensive, I got traded to the New York Mets. I wound up M.V.P. of the World Series, something Clemente and Stargell would also be. So the third, fourth, and fifth hitters in our old Pirates' lineup all turned out to be M.V.P.'s in the World Series!

The 1969 Mets were a very sound club – study history and you'll find that good defense and good pitching is always going to win out over a bombarding offense.

The Mets had great young arms and a good defensive team. All they needed was some timely hitting; I was able to help supply that throughout the year. The first few games in a row with the Mets, I drove in the tying or the winning run. That, and the fact I was older than most of my teammates, made me a leader immediately.

The Mets had party records going and comedians coming in the clubhouse before games. We found out what breaks tension – laughter.

* * * * *

I stressed what I call second career first. Baseball can get rid of us. We have to have something to fall back on. Black players in particular: there were not many back then just sitting on the bench. Either you played or you're gone.

After baseball, I was still with General Electric in New York, then I went to the Mead Corporation. I left there to resume law school, then took a job for eighteen months at DAP, a division of DAP spackling compound. They wanted a personnel department built from scratch. Later on, I was CEO of Chicago Economic Development.

Then a group conceived the idea of a formal winter baseball league with the hope, after three years of international play, of converting to a third major league. FOX Television was interested in sponsoring the league. I was going to be Acting Commissioner of that league for the first two or three years; once it converted, there would be another Commissioner. For headquarters we chose South Dakota, because it has no personal income tax and no corporate tax.

In inclement weather areas, we would play in indoor stadiums. We had fourteen teams in places like Tokyo, Taiwan, Vancouver, Montreal, Toronto. Donald Trump, Joe Robbie and others were interested backers.

Anyway, it fell through. I decided to stay in South Dakota and I've been here ever since.

Looking back, I had wanted to be baseball's second black General Manager. I wanted to go in somebody's organization and learn, but I never got the opportunity.

I had always set my sights high. At Morehouse College back in the early '50s, a recent graduate would help acclimate you to Morehouse. Martin Luther King, Jr. was my "big brother." Martin was a great guy. I knew the whole King family. Christine and I taught at the same elementary school.

Morehouse was an academic college. Athletics was incidental. I was All-American in three sports and the President there didn't even know it. All he knew was I was on the honor roll. At Morehouse, we made up our minds that we were going to try to get blacks in positions they had not been in before. My classmate, Maynard Jackson, was the first black mayor of Atlanta.

* * * * *

Returning to Maz: he made so many great plays, I was always in awe. Dive to his right, dive to his left. Maz knew how to play hitters and he was smart. He had a sixth sense about what was going to happen next.

Maz belongs in the Hall of Fame. You can't show me a better second baseman. I've seen them all from the '50s, so you've got to go back a long way to show me a better second baseman than Bill Mazeroski.

Bill was a great player on the field and a great person off the field. He never had a cruel word or an unkind word to say to anyone. If Maz couldn't say something positive and pleasant, he wouldn't say anything at all.

To know Maz is to love Maz.

"If you put Maz on any team, you'd make it a much better club. Maz was a leader – on and off the field."

– Richie Hebner

18

Richie Hebner

Richie Hebner played third base for the Pittsburgh Pirates from 1968-1976, then played with the Phillies in '77 and '78, the Mets in '79, the Tigers, '80-'82, the Pirates again in '82-'83, and the Cubs, '83-'84. Richie played infield, outfield, and was a designated hitter for Detroit. Hebner holds the National League record for most appearances in a League Championship Series – 8. Hebner's Pirates made the playoffs in '70, '71, '72, '74, and '75, as did his Phillies in '77 and '78 and Cubs in '84. A Massachusetts high school hockey star, Richie dug graves in baseball's off-season to stay in shape. He hit .300 twice and played seventeen seasons in the major leagues. Richie is now the manager of the Syracuse Chiefs of the International League.

I started skating when I was six years old. High school hockey would draw five thousand people. High school baseball would draw fifteen people. So hockey was my big thing.

A lot of people wanted me to sign with the Boston Bruins. I had a chance to sign with the Detroit Red Wings, but I ended up the number one pick for the Pittsburgh Pirates in 1966, the sixteenth pick in the country.

I played three years in the minors and by my third year I was in the big leagues. I made the right decision. But I always think I would like to have tried the N.H.L...imagine being on the Boston Bruins with Bobby Orr, Phil Esposito, Derek Sanderson! I still skate in the winter. Hockey, if you give someone an elbow, you only get penalized two minutes. You do that in baseball, they'll throw you out for a week. I enjoyed playing hockey more than I enjoyed playing baseball.

Al Oliver and I got called up on the same day from Columbus, Ohio, the last three weeks of the '68 season. I was so green, a twenty-year-old kid from Boston, talking funny. Pittsburgh people would ask me, "What are you saying? Are you related to the Kennedys or something?"

I sat on the bench those last three weeks, and I was in awe. In the dressing room there was Stargell's locker, Mazeroski's locker, Clemente's locker, and my locker. I was two years out of high school. In 1969, the Pirates went with three rookies: Al Oliver, Manny Sanguillen, and me.

Maz saved me a lot of errors. You'd like to get a ground ball at third and throw right to his chest. But I would throw balls down in the dirt, I'd throw balls up, and he'd still turn them over. I thought, "I'd better start throwing balls at his chest because I'm going to get this thirty-two-year-old guy killed one night and I'm going to feel bad about it." Whenever I threw to second for a double play, if the ball was bad, Maz would still make the pivot look easy.

In the dugout I'd say, "Maz, that was a great play." He'd say, "Hey, kid, I've been doing that for a lot of years. Don't feel bad."

Mazeroski's glove looked like a Little League glove. An old Little League glove. When you have good hands, you can use anything.

Maz was a natural. Like Larry Bird. He didn't run fast, he wasn't fancy. Maz batted eighth one year, 1962, and had eighty-some RBI's. Do you know how incredible that is? Think of it.

When I came up, Stargell would talk, Mazeroski would talk, Clemente, Clendenon. That's a problem nowadays. Rookies come up and big leaguers give them a semi-cold shoulder.

If any of those veterans had ever yelled at me, my career would have ended. But they were so nice to me.

I weighed 185, 190 when I came up. Down from 215 in high school. That was probably just baby fat. I lost that in the Marine Corps.

Joe Brown, the Pirates' GM, came down to Johnson City, Tennessee one night. He put his arm around Bob Moose and me and said, "You two are going to be in Parris Island next week." As any eighteen-year-old kid from Boston might put it, I said, "Where the hell is Parris Island?" Boy, I found out where Parris Island was.

Back then, Pittsburgh had two openings in the reserves, for two guys they'd think might make the big leagues. Other than that, it was two years – one year in Vietnam. And you don't know if you're going to come back with a tag on your toe or not.

I had no idea I was going to play seventeen years in the big leagues. But I did. I have the National League record of eight playoff appearances. Actually I've been in nine – one as a coach with the Red Sox. Nine playoffs. Unfortunately, we lost eight of them. That's a bad percentage, isn't it?

When we lost on the wild pitch in the 1972 playoffs with Cincinnati, that was the toughest loss I had in the big leagues. In Riverfront Stadium, you walk from the field, down the steps, long runway, up the steps. After the wild pitch, that walk back to the clubhouse felt like a twenty-two-dollar cab ride. We didn't know it, but that was Clemente's last game.

Clemente's throws to third were always around the base. I played four years with Roberto. Like Maz, he made very few mental mistakes. Also like Maz, he got very little recognition playing in the small market of Pittsburgh. I mean, I hit .301 my rookie year at Pittsburgh, 1969. Four hundred and fifty at-bats. Never got a vote for Rookie of the Year! I always won-dered about that. Teddy Sizemore won it that season with L.A.

Maz was quiet. But he was great with his teammates. You watched the way Maz played, and you tried to play like him. Maz wasn't Knute Rockne. He'd just say, "I'll play a hundred and forty games, bust my tail, get flipped a few times in dou-ble plays, get a few black and blues on my shins, but I'll play." To see a guy like him, thirty-three years old – and I'm twenty?? Shit, if he can do it, you know the hell I'm going to do it. If you didn't try to play as hard as Maz, you were stupid.

The older guys like Maz influenced the young puppies com-ing up. The Pirates had a good combination.

Practical jokes stick in your mind. I threw a helmet once; next day I come to the ballpark, I get a Western Union. It looked legit to me – five-hundred-dollar fine. I'm making ten thousand dollars in 1969, the minimum. Five-hundred-dollar fine, signed "Chub Feeney," President of the National League. I think Maz and Jim Bunning were behind it. They didn't let me know for about a day.

The Pirates were some kind of team. If you didn't hit .300 in Pittsburgh, you were absolutely embarrassed. Hitting was contagious. We got in very few slumps.

The 1971 Series was a special time. I was a twenty-three-year-old kid, four years in the big leagues, and here I had a World Series ring. Think of the great players who never get to even appear in a Series – like Ernie Banks.

* * * * *

I was about the only guy on the Pirates who was single. I wasn't Saint Richard. But you can imagine what the papers would print. I'm here, there, everywhere. Actually I was kind of a homebody. I lived at home until I was thirty-three years old, when I got married. My father owned a cemetery and I've been helping him dig graves for the last twenty-five years. Pick and shovel. No backhoe.

I grew up with no sisters. There were five Hebner brothers. Half a baseball team. We'd go to the playgrounds and, hell, we'd only need four more guys to make a team. Now look at the playgrounds during the summer. Empty. No pick-up games anymore.

When I was growing up, certainly when Maz was growing up, it was, "I'm going to the baseball field, Mom. Ring the cowbell and I'll be home when supper's ready." That's the way it was.

I had fun playing a year and a half in Forbes Field. But the new ballpark was nice. I got the first hit at Three Rivers Stadium. That night Dock Ellis pitched and we lost 3-2. But I got the first hit and the first RBI at Three Rivers.

Like I tell the Blue Jay kids, time goes so quickly. It's as if I was just putting the uniform on, Opening Day at Busch Stadium, 1969, against Bob Gibson. Next thing I know, Jimmy Frey of the Cubs is calling me into his office in Mesa, Arizona in March, '85: "We're going to release you." Boom!

So I tell these kids, "Give it everything you've got. No matter what happens, you can go home to your friends, your girl-friend, your wife, look yourself in the mirror, and say, 'I tried.'" Besides, they're giving away money in the big leagues!

What do you think Maz would be making in 1995 if he was playing second base the way he could? Damn good money. Because defense wins every kind of game. Hockey, basketball, football, baseball. If you can't win those 2-1, 3-2 games, you'll be watching the playoffs in your living room instead of from the field.

* * * * *

The game has changed. Defense is easier on artificial turf than on grass. The turf is flatter! But now bunting has gone down the drain. Aaron, Mays, even Dave Kingman could bunt. Steve Garvey, too.

When I played third, and I'd see Garvey up, I'd think, "I don't want to be drinking out of a straw for two months." I got my teeth lost in hockey once. I didn't want to lose them again.

When you play on turf and it's been raining or it's wet, and that ball hits that turf...try to stop it. You don't know if it's going to hit your glove, your shin, or your mouth. It's tough.

Richie Hebner leaps to catch a wide throw from Manny Sanguillen, as Joe Morgan steals third

And going into Riverfront Stadium watching those righthanded sluggers coming up. Bench, Perez, Foster – geez.

Maz and Alley both had great range to their right. That made a huge difference, because I could play closer to the line. Over a hundred and sixty-two games I could get to more balls, thanks to them. And Maz really knew how to play hitters, which takes awhile. Billy Williams up, play here; Ernie Banks, over there.

Maz played hard, I tell you. His body was beaten up when I got there. His legs were killing him, he had arm problems. But such a great guy to be around. Never got loud.

Even when Maz didn't play, players knew he was in the dugout, watching. You'd make a good stop, and two innings later he'd say, "That's a nice play you made." It really meant something, coming from a guy with eight Gold Gloves. That's eight more than I had.

He was the fastest I ever saw at second base with the pivot. "Just get me the ball in time, and we'll make this double play." I made some bad throws to Maz, who got flipped a couple of times, but I don't ever remember Maz saying, "Don't do that again, kid." He helped my confidence.

And I saw him at the end of his career! His legs were black and blue. He reminded me of a goalie in the National Hockey League. But you couldn't knock him down. Sliding into him at second base was like hitting an oak tree.

Maz was so valuable in the field. Plus, he was a tough out. What's more, he was a good family man. If anybody ever made a bad comment about Maz, I would have that fellow investigated by the F.B.I.

Maz's defensive numbers are some pretty good numbers for upstate New York, I think.

*   *   *   *   *

I played with the Mets in 1979 and we did not draw a million people in New York City! We had ninety-nine losses with eight games to go in the season. We sweep the Cubs four straight. Go to St. Louis, sweep them four straight. We're flying back to LaGuardia. Our manager, Joe Torre, stands up and says, "Christ, now you guys get hot." We couldn't even lose a hundred games!

Speaking of managers on plane trips, Danny Murtaugh would read cowboy books. About 120 pages, he'd read one in two hours. Danny would fall asleep. Our announcer, Bob Prince, would sneak up, take the book from his hand, rip the last fifteen pages out, and put it back in his hand. Danny would wake up from his nap, flying to L.A. or somewhere. He couldn't finish the book. Fun to watch.

I left Pittsburgh as one of the first free agents. I played in Philadelphia and had two good years. We got in the playoffs twice.

They traded me to the New York Mets. Nino Espinosa for me. I went from a first-place team to a team that came in last.

Went from Veterans Stadium, forty thousand, and loud, to Shea Stadium, quiet as my father's cemetery. Getting traded is part of baseball. But when that happened, it was tough. I rented a house at Cedarhurst, Long Island. Left at 2:30 in the afternoon just to beat the traffic when games were still 8:00 pm.

Looking back on my career, one highlight was hitting for the cycle. It was the funniest thing. I needed a home run my last time up. So I hit one inside the park. That was like hitting the lottery.

I had a couple of five for five games. But not back to back. I saw Clemente get five hits in Dodger Stadium one night. The next night, five more hits. Ten for thirteen in two games. Not bad!

Clemente had been in a slump going into the series with the Dodgers. Tony Bartirome, the trainer, said, "I'm going to get you out of this slump." He gave Clemente a back rub with skim milk. I'm going, "Tony, what the hell are you doing?" Clemente was superstitious. He got his back rubbed: five hits. Tony had to go out and buy more skim milk, so Roberto could get another five the next game. That's a true story.

I was there the night Stargell hit the first home run out of Dodger Stadium. Right center. There was a kid walking out with his father about the seventh inning. They leave a little early in Dodger Stadium. The kid brought the ball in the clubhouse two nights later and Willie signed it.

I've always wondered, when a guy hits a home run, why does the next guy have to get drilled? I batted behind Willie and I would get drilled. I'd say, "Willie, why are you hitting these monsters? I've got black and blues all over my body. You're killing me."

After I retired, I managed Myrtle Beach in the Sally League, in 1988. Then I was the Red Sox hitting coach in '89, '90, and '91. Our manager, Joe Morgan, and all of us got fired. I called about sixteen teams in 1992. I couldn't get a job. I just laid low.

Since 1993 I've been a minor league hitting coach and manager for the Blue Jays, one of the finest organizations in baseball. They care about their kids. The organization is first class.

It really is fun going to the ballpark. I've been down in the Instructional League for seven weeks now this fall. It's fun watching these kids improve.

Getting back to Maz – he would always be in the right position as a cutoff man. He was not a fancy guy, just a blue collar ballplayer. He was brought up that way to show up every day. When he didn't play, you knew he was hurting.

Maz was a great guy who gave you one hundred percent. If you put Maz on any team, you'd make it a much better club. Maz was a leader – on and off the field.

I saw him at the end of his career when he was beaten up a bit. Some games, you knew he was suffering. But Maz went out there and busted his tail. Always.

*"**F**or me it was a dream come true to play with Bill Mazeroski."*

– Manny Sanguillen

19

Manny Sanguillen

Manny Sanguillen has the highest lifetime batting average of any catcher of the post-World War II era. Manny hit .296, bettering Thurman Munson's .292, Yogi Berra's .285, Roy Campanella's .276, and Johnny Bench's .267. Manny hit .300 four times in thirteen years. He has two World Series rings, from 1971 and 1979, and was named an All-Star in '71, '72, and '75. Sanguillen began his career with Pittsburgh in 1967; he was their starting catcher from '69 to '76. Traded to Oakland in '76, Manny returned to close out his career with the Pirates from '78 to '80. Extremely fast for a catcher (he hit 57 triples, including three with the bases loaded in 1971), Manny anchored Pirate teams that appeared in the playoffs five times in six years. Manny lives in Boca Raton, Florida, and works with Champions Management.

I was born in Colon, Panama, in 1944. Rod Carew, one of the greatest hitters ever, was born there too, but he went to New York at an early age. I remember 1960 when Mazeroski hit the home run to beat the Yankees. People in Panama really liked Roberto Clemente and his team because we were a Spanish country.

Growing up, I boxed. I wanted to make a living. I outgrew the 140 pound weight class, went right past 185 and was out of boxing.

But it helped me to be flexible, move quickly, and stay low. That's the way I used to catch.

I never played baseball until I was 19 years old. I learned to catch six weeks before I came to the United States, in 1965. No experience, so no pressure!

Herbert Rayburn signed me. He is from Panama. He worked me hard and taught me good habits. I thank God I listened to what he said.

From the very beginning I'd swing at anything and I'd make contact. It's a gift. I never saw Yogi Berra play, but everybody would tell me I was the best bad-ball hitter since Yogi.

I played my first year in the minors in New York, then I went to Raleigh, North Carolina, for my second year. From there Columbus, Ohio, and the year after, the big leagues, in 1967.

The first pitcher that I faced was a fat guy named Dave Giusti of the Houston Astros. My first hit was an infield hit, a ground ball to second base to Joe Morgan, a three-bouncer. I beat Joe's throw to first base. He was mad.

* * * * *

When Maz was playing he was all grace and concentration. He knew how to play every hitter on every single team. When the ball went to Bill, I knew we had an out, especially on the double play. It made you feel good. The pitchers and I would try to make batters hit ground balls his way. Especially with men on base.

To this day, I can't figure out how Maz could be so quick throwing the ball from second base. And how many guys he used to stop with his strong legs – the runners would hit him and bounce back! I played with him from 1967 to 1972. You know, Joe Morgan said that Mazeroski was an inspiration to him.

To be as durable as Maz, you had to be almost superhuman, with some kind of courage, determination, and toughness inside.

I remember when I first came into the Pirate clubhouse, Bill Mazeroski saw me and said, "I like you." Maz said to me, "I see a lot of guys coming and going and I don't want you to go."

Early in the morning, when we would all go out to eat breakfast, everybody ordered eggs, or milk and oatmeal. Mazeroski would ask for two Budweisers and two large Kielbasa sausages at 8:00 in the morning. I never saw that before. I thought it was the greatest thing ever.

Bill was always there at the right time when you needed him. He never had a bad temper. Bill Mazeroski and Roberto Clemente were great influences on me. Fine leaders.

I never saw Bill thrown out of a game. He always showed appreciation and love for the game, for the Pittsburgh Pirates and for Pittsburgh. And today Bill Mazeroski is the same as he was before.

Maz has a good sense of humor. I remember we were in Panama in 1971. Maz was introduced to the crowd first; then Roberto Clemente came in, and the crowd started to go crazy. So Mazeroski tells me and Clemente, "Man, these people in Panama love me!" But you know, those people did like Bill Mazeroski. That standing ovation was for him too.

In the field, Maz stayed low with great body control, great balance. He was like a tiger. He got a very good push-off when he wanted to go to second base to make the double play. That first step was fast. Then the pivot – the ball just went bing! and people said, "Wow, how can he do that?" Joe Morgan is right: Bill Mazeroski was an inspiration. He is in my Hall of Fame. Bill was blessed from God to show compassion and respect and he treated you like you were the greatest. That is rare.

* * * * *

The toughest play for the catcher happens when you have men on first and second base and there is a ground ball; sometimes you are tempted to leave home plate alone. If you do that, somebody has to back you up. Otherwise, the runner goes to third and keeps going to home plate. You have to make sure that you and the pitcher know what to do.

Throwing out the runner trying to steal second was easiest for me on a slider a little bit to the right of home plate. You are right there, ready to throw.

I used to have a hard time throwing the ball to third base, but nobody ever stole home on me. A couple of people tried. Some guy with the Chicago Cubs tried me three times and didn't cross home plate. I pretended like I didn't see him, but I was watching!

At the plate, pitchers knocked me down a lot, but that made me a better hitter. My bat wasn't the heaviest, but I have to say it was the longest: 37 inches long.

They called me "Crazy Legs" – I had to learn not to run through the bases – and "Roadrunner" too. I was the first Roadrunner, before Ralph Garr. And I think I was the fastest catcher of all time.

Not everyone knows that I had the highest career batting average, .296, of any catcher in my lifetime. That statistic is the kind of thing that people forget about with Spanish players. We love this country and we love the fans, but the writers do forget about us. Johnny Bench, Thurman Munson, Yogi Berra, Roy Campanella, those are pretty good guys to have behind you in career batting average.

I threw out my share of base-stealers, too. I don't think there are too many people who threw Lou Brock out twice in one game. I did. Lou and I would battle.

Brock was a little scared of Bob Veale sometimes because Bob was nearsighted and would take off his glasses and pitch anyway.

Willie McCovey too. One day Bob Veale took those glasses off and threw the ball 100 miles per hour at McCovey. I asked Veale what happened and he said, "My glasses were too wet and I wanted to show him I could throw a strike without my glasses." That ball thrown at McCovey was 10 feet high.

I caught one no-hitter, thrown by Bobby Moose against the incredible '69 New York Mets, in September when they were hot. We swept that series. That's when I knew we were going to have a good team.

In 1970 I was in Miami on the way to Panama, watching the World Series in the airport and I thought, "That is going to be us next year." We won the Series the next year. That season the Pirates never lost concentration, or our faith in each other.

The next season ended with a loss to the Reds in the 1972 playoffs. That wild pitch from Moose, a slider, was a bad pitch.

After the wild pitch ended the game, everybody was around my locker; I told all the sportswriters I'd tried to catch the ball.

After the '72 season I spent a couple more years with the Pirates, then went to Oakland in '76. I was traded for a manager, Chuck Tanner. The next year, on the last day of spring

Celebrating a Game 7 victory with Steve Blass in 1971: "The Pirates never lost concentration, or our faith in each other"

training, Oakland traded me for five or six guys back to Pittsburgh!

I did get another World Series ring in 1979, but the one reason I wanted to come back to Pittsburgh is I loved the city, the people and the Pirates. When I came back the fans gave me a tremendous standing ovation. I started to cry deep in my heart.

I used to live in Pittsburgh. I used to go to homes, to the Y.M.C.A., Catholic churches, in every part of Pittsburgh to speak to the fans. I wanted to give something back.

Some seasons 500 kids waited for me at Three Rivers by my car in the middle of June or July. I signed autographs for every one. Michael Moorer, a former heavyweight champion boxer, is from Pennsylvania. In the '70s he was a kid in Pittsburgh, and one night, the only player who signed an autograph for him was me; Michael told me he would never forget that.

* * * * *

The Pittsburgh Pirates were people who would fight for each other. We were a family. Clemente, then Willie Stargell, kept it going. Even today, when I visit the ghettos of Chicago and Los Angeles, young kids ask me about Roberto Clemente. They want to know. I tell them I was blessed to play with Roberto.

Today I represent mostly Latin baseball players as an agent here in Boca Raton. Orlando Merced, Julio Franco, Chico Lind, Luis Polonia, Javier Lopez, Stanley Javier, to name a few. Every one of my players will hopefully save money and be prepared. When they get out of the game they will have something.

To this day I consider Maz the greatest second baseman I ever saw. People should read about Maz, find out about all the things he did on the field, his movements, his confidence, the way he positioned himself going for the ball. For me it was a dream come true to play with Bill Mazeroski.

"You would like to have 25 guys like Maz and you could sleep good every night."

– Harry Walker

20

Harry Walker

Harry "The Hat" Walker (so named because of his habit of fidgeting with his cap before each at-bat) belongs to quite a baseball family. His father, Dixie, once roomed with Walter Johnson while pitching for the Washington Senators; his uncle Ernie was a St. Louis Browns outfielder; Harry's brother, also named Dixie, won a National League batting title, as did Harry, who hit .296 for the Cardinals, Phillies, and Cubs over 11 years. An All-Star outfielder in '43 and '47, Harry went on to manage at St. Louis, Pittsburgh and Houston. Born in 1918, Harry still teaches hitting to young ballplayers.

Bill was the best double play man that I have managed or seen. He got the ball coming off the bag, which I liked very much because you get the ball sooner. Your foot is turning and you come off that bag towards first base. Maz was terrific at handling the ball. The key to it was getting there early enough so that he could control the ball. Wherever the ball was, his right foot had to go and the left foot had to swing over then to first base, which I've got pictures of here that I took. I show them to all the kids throughout the country.

Maz took the ball ninety percent of the time with his right foot coming off the bag anchored and the left foot in the air. And he got the ball on the other side of the bag, not on this side and step back. There's got to be a step and a half to two steps' difference in Maz's style and anybody else who takes their foot and comes back. He got rid of it so quick.

I'll never forget a game at Houston. We had a big six- or seven-run lead and the inning's about over, game's about over. Get on the bus, let's go. It wound up with bases loaded, the tying run on third and one out. Ball is hit past the third baseman and I thought sure it was through for a base hit. The winning run is on second. Gene Alley at short took the ball into him in one motion prior to Maz getting it. It looked like it richocheted off Maz's glove. Maz threw the guy out by a good step. Greatest double play I ever saw. Our dugout was halfway mystified, I guess. Everybody was excited and that's the best I ever saw a double play made.

To make the double play you've got to cheat a little bit. You've got to know your hitters. And you've got to get in position early enough so you get that ball and get out before you get racked. They hit Maz occasionally, not much. But he'd come right up over the top of them. He got rid of the ball so fast and had such good hands, good reflexes. A strong individual.

Maz was also a pretty good hitter. Got a lot of big hits, drove in a lot of runs, plenty in the years I was there. They had a great double play combination, he and Alley. They set the record. I'll never forget that one in Houston. It looked like it bounced off a wall.

Maz just did his thing on the field. He never got involved with anything. He was a nice guy. Never got in an argument with anybody hardly. Just went about his work.

You would like to have 25 guys like Maz and you could sleep good every night. That's the best way I can put it. Did his job and did it well.

At first Joe Morgan couldn't make a double play. I let him look at Maz – when I first went to Houston, writers swore Joe would never turn seven double plays from his side but he turned out to be a real good double play man. He learned to do what Maz did, take the ball coming across the bag.

Morgan got hit one time by turning. That woke him up. Joe learned to open that leg up instead of having it anchored sideways and getting hit. Get that ball and get it out of there like Maz did.

Jackie Robinson was an all-around strong ballplayer. But he never was the fielder Maz was. I don't know of anybody who was. Mazeroski was strong, graceful, quick. The ball hit his glove and it was gone. He didn't drop his arm and wind up to throw. If he caught it up above his head, it went from there. If he caught it at the belt it went from there.

* * * * *

Forbes Field had a hard rough infield. The ball bounced pretty bad. You didn't have the grass of today or Astroturf. Maz got down soon enough so when the ball'd come up, he'd come up. When the ball was about ten feet away he got down low, feet apart, right foot back, left foot extended, and he caught the ball, brought it right in and from there it was gone. He's the best I ever saw. Why not copy him? That's like hitters: Why not copy Ted Williams, Musial, Aaron, guys that really pounded the ball and hit for an average?

Fielding today is outstanding. The big glove makes the difference. It used to be the first baseman had a big glove and nobody else was allowed to use them. Now everybody's got a first baseman's glove. It's supposed to be no more than 12 inches but some of them go 14, 15 inches. It's a big web you sweep. That's bound to take hits away from the hitters.

A rain delay at Forbes Field gives Harry Walker the chance to elaborate on his favorite subject: baseball

I see a lot of outfielders run by and catch the ball on the side, run three steps, transfer it to their hand, then turn to throw. Rico Carty started that mess. He used to catch every ball on the glove side. Terrible outfielder, great hitter. Now if a guy catches the ball, runs with it and transfers it to the other hand, he's letting that runner take two or three steps tagging up. Instead of getting the ball here, and throw, it's here, run, run, throw.

Like the double play we talked about. The longer I take to get rid of that ball, if I catch it and drop my hands...see, Maz never dropped his hands to wind up to throw. He got rid of the ball all in one motion. The best I ever saw. The man was just amazing.

Ground balls were hit, he'd break real hard. When the ball was about ten feet in front, he'd be right down there with the glove on the ground with his rear end under him low, and bring the ball right up. He never was off balance. He broke hard, ran hard, then got set to field the ball.

He didn't run over it or stumble up. Had the surest hands of anybody I've seen. Nobody can touch him today.

There are some great fielders now. Fielding is as good as I've ever seen it. Only thing is the Astroturf; the fields are manicured. The Cardinals' field in 1942 had no grass on the infield. They sprayed it green. And rocks! The outfield didn't get watered much because they were afraid it would rain. It was cracked out there, your spikes would get hung up. Balls were bound to take off and you had to learn to get set, be quick with your hands. Today it's a pool table.

By the time we played the 1942 World Series, the field had been used so much the Cardinals had to bring somebody to spray-paint the damn infield. It had no grass. The Browns played and we played. Branch Rickey, the Cardinals' GM, would have tryouts at 6:00 or 8:00 in the morning, as long as they'd let him, then the ball club would play. So the field never got a chance to rest.

When it rained, out would come the old canvas, so big it took twenty guys. Occasionally one of them would fall and it'd almost kill him before they could get him out from under it.

Today they are bringing players up in two, three years; they never learned to play, a lot of them. I played two years in Triple A ball. Had a great year the first year. Hit over .300 as a leadoff man, hit 17 home runs, had thirty some-odd doubles, drove in seventy runs in 125 games, big for a leadoff man. But they had other ballplayers up there so they would push you back another time.

I've been lucky to play on winners. I played in three World Series and we won two of them. Played in three Little World Series and we won all three of them.

My biggest thrill was being able to manage people like Mazeroski, Stargell and Clemente. I had Musial and Schoendienst, Ken Boyer. I had some great ones.

Bill Mazeroski ought to be in the Hall of Fame. Best damn second baseman I ever saw, and I saw some good ones. Schoendienst. Schoendienst is in there – but he couldn't play second base like Mazeroski. He hit better. But that gets you in the Hall of Fame more than anything else. You hit and you go. You don't hit, you don't go. That's why shortstops, not many make it, though the guy with St. Louis now [Ozzie Smith] will.

Johnny Mize was a great hitter but he couldn't run, couldn't throw, couldn't field. You sure didn't pay him a dollar for fielding. Ralph Kiner, terrible outfielder. He couldn't run. But he could hit and that's what puts you there. Second base and shortstop should be under a different category. They are the play-makers.

*   *   *   *   *

Yes, Alley and Maz at short and second made the game easy. Clendenon at first base wasn't bad. He did have one bad habit – when he got the ground ball and the runner went to second he'd hit him in the back! If he threw five times, two or three hit the runner. He wouldn't step way inside to throw or step back, he'd just get it and whirl.

Throwing right for the bag you're gonna hit him. But that's the only bad thing Clendenon did. He did a good job, hit a lot of home runs, had lots of RBI's.

They're getting to the point now they're cheating the game. What are they going to do this year? Wild card. Eight clubs playing for the championship! All of a sudden a team finishes fast, gets hot and beats everybody else, it goes to the World Series. And it didn't play .500 ball!

The World Series is not going to be a classic anymore. They're gonna wind up with clubs that get hot that have a lousy record and win the whole thing. I just won 98 ballgames, you won 65, and you're representing us in the World Series? It's gonna kill the goose that laid the golden egg.

*   *   *   *   *

Every man has got to learn to do what he can do, work hard to improve himself. Hell, I started out when my Dad was running the ballgame at the coal mines in Sipsey, Alabama.

Those were tough times in the '20s. Breakfast a lot of times was milk gravy made from powdered milk. It wasn't milk, it was powder with water mixed. And the gravy wasn't made with white meat, it was fatback.

We took the grease and salt and pepper and flour and milk made up out of water, and whipped that up for breakfast along with toast. Not toast but biscuits – we didn't have toast, didn't have white bread. And we had it better than most folks did.

Don't tell me football is a bigger game, that's a lot of crap. I like football too, but it's not outdrawing baseball. You let those guys play for five and a half months every day and tell me how many people are going to support them.

I loved every day I played. I got tired but if I had it to do over I'd give anything in the world to do it again. I hated to quit at 41 when I was playing in the minor leagues.

Stan Musial today would probably not play big league ball. Why? He started out as a pitcher; hurt his arm and couldn't throw. The Cardinals took a look at Stan in 1941. Going north my first year, the Cardinals played against the Columbus, Georgia farm team, with Musial pitching. And we hit him pretty hard. Terry Moore, Johnny Mize were hitting home runs off of him. "Man, I'd love to hit against you for a living." Stan just laughed. But that was it, he was through. Then somebody said he's a pretty good athlete. They found a place to play him in the outfield, Springfield, Missouri, Class C. Stan hit well there, got promoted to Rochester, then made the Cardinals for good that September.

Today they don't have that. They release players and don't let them go to bat fifty times. Stan Musial would have been released because he couldn't pitch. They wouldn't bother with him today because they'd have other guys who can run and throw too and they're letting a lot of them go. Now, the "stars" you put $200,000 or $300,000 into, they're going to play. But that guy signing up to play like I did, like Musial did, wouldn't. Let the "stars" play: they've got to come through or the team looks foolish.

Hell, in 1938 I got $150 a month in Montgomery. Got hit in the Adam's apple. Then I had a hernia split and I wouldn't tell. At the end of 1938, the Phillies drafted me from

Montgomery. They cut me from $150 to $125 a month. The next year they sent me a contract to report. If I hadn't loved the game, I would have quit before playing one minute in the major leagues. After the year I had, getting whacked, with my appendix ruptured the year before. I could have said, oh, to hell with it. But I wanted to play bad enough.

I was a very lucky individual. I liked the game, loved to play it, fought hard to play it. You've got to have a strong desire for anything, baseball or anything, to succeed at it. If you're not willing to pay the price, you're not gonna make it.

The first thing I do with teaching these real young kids, I say, I don't want you to sit here and piddle around and not pay attention – then I'm wasting my time and yours, too. And then they come alive.

"It was such a good feeling to be on a team with a guy who you have so much confidence in that you never thought he would miss a ball or throw a ball away."

– Alex Grammas

21

Alex Grammas

As a slick-fielding rookie shortstop in 1954, Alex Grammas was the second-best fielder in the National League, behind his Cardinal teammate, Hall of Famer Red Schoendienst, according to *Total Baseball*. Alex played ten years with the Cardinals, Reds, and Cubs, managed the Pirates and the Milwaukee Brewers, and coached for the Pirates, Reds, and Tigers.

When I started out, I spent five years in the minor leagues as a player before I came to the major leagues. In those days it was more the rule than the exception to the rule, but I think we learned how to play the game a little better than the kids today because they do have a tendency to rush them. Some teams like the Cardinals, they had 26, 28 minor league teams. Now a team may have five or six. Makes a big difference. By staying back and playing more minor league baseball you learned the game.

When you get to the major leagues for the first time, you're real antsy. Jittery. This is what you've been working for and you feel like you've got the confidence.

But you're not quite sure. Some kids who did well in the minor leagues could never beat it between the ears. Some guys, just the opposite – in the majors, mentally they were tougher and got things rolling in their favor.

I can remember going to spring training my first year [1954], Eddie Stanky was the manager of the Cardinals. Watching guys like Red Schoendienst and Stan Musial walk into the clubhouse. You're not saying anything because you're just a new kid on the block. But you're not missing anything either. You're talking to yourself: Do I belong here? I'm going to show these guys that I do.

The first time you go to bat in a major league game your knees are knocking. That first ground ball hit to you...you want to make sure everything goes right. It's not hard to remember at all. These kids today go through the same thing. You try to be tolerant, patient. Because you know what they're going through. It's easier for them if they get encouragement. Guys tried to help me – you just try to pass that along. Once the games get going, you get used to it and it works out. It's a funny thing but it does, it works out.

When I first started playing, fielders were still leaving their gloves on the field. As soon as the inning was over you came in – if you had to charge a ball on the infield grass and throw the guy out and it would be the third out, you'd just sail your glove back behind shortstop or something. Lot of guys would stuff tobacco in the other guy's finger. It's better with them off the field. When they changed that custom, it was a little tough to get out of the habit. You'd find yourself throwing the thing and then having to run out to get it. Just about ready to sail it and you'd say uh-oh and you'd put it in your hand, you know.

Umpires? When I started they didn't wear glasses, though some of them needed to. Umpires have a tough job. We have a home town we can settle in. They don't. They all try hard, give it the best shot they know how. When you get to know them you find out they're as human as anyone else. They tell jokes and play golf, too.

Forbes Field. I used to love Forbes Field. Real short porch in right field down the line. The fence went real deep to right center where there was one of those rolling iron gates to I think 433 in center and then came back around to the scoreboard, I think around 360.

So much tradition. And you were pretty close to the people when I was coaching there. You felt like you were sitting right in the box seats with them.

Fielders today, I see more guys using one hand; infielders try to backhand balls when they should be trying to get in front of them. And throwing on the run, much more than they used to.

One of my pet peeves is a second baseman or shortstop taking a throw from the catcher. Get the bag between your legs! Don't get up in front of the bag and take the throw. Because when you reach out in front of you to take the throw from the catcher, and the bag is back here, by the time you take it and reach here, you lose a lot of guys who are stealing bases. If you get the bag between your legs and you wait for the ball to come, all you have to do is catch the ball and drop your hand. It's so much quicker it's not even funny.

If a ball beats the runner, generally they're going to call him out. But a lot of times you miss the guy because you weren't able to make it close. Sometimes guys think that they might get hurt, with a guy that slides hard. Frank Robinson, Willie Mays used to slide hard. You do have a chance of getting hurt but that's part of the game. The object is to try to get the guy out.

And know when to throw it and when not to throw it! I've seen so many balls thrown away because a guy had no chance at all and ended up throwing the ball in the dugout. We've all done it. I've done it.

Slow-hit ball to the first baseman. That's a tough ball to make a double play on to begin with. The ball is topped to the first baseman and he fires it to you. Somebody's got to be covering first on it; he might not be able to get back just right. The pitcher is going to be crossing over. You're going to try to hit a moving target. Nine times out of ten you better stick that ball in your pocket. You'll see guys invariably throw that ball away. They'll throw that thing in the dugout or against the fence and it's just uncalled for.

On the double play at second, I think the fielder shouldn't have to hang around the bag. That action happens so fast sometimes it tricks the umpire. Doesn't realize it until after he's called the guy out. And watch out for the second baseman who straddles the bag when he takes the throw. I've seen a lot of them straddle that bag, catch and throw the ball, and never even touch the bag!

Another pet peeve involving infielders: a slow-hit ball that they try to barehand. If that ball is rolling, I say catch it with your glove. If the ball is at a dead stop, I say pick it up with your bare hand.

You don't get rid of the ball any quicker by barehanding it than you do by catching it in your glove. Because as you catch it in your glove you're coming back anyway. I could come in on a ball as good as any human. And I never barehanded a ball in my life that wasn't sitting still.

You can't throw the ball until your right leg gets around anyway. You have to catch the ball with your left foot forward. If I catch the ball with my right foot forward, then my left foot is going to have to hit and my right foot is going to have to hit before I can throw.

Well, it's easy to talk about Bill Mazeroski. He's such a nice person. Not only a hell of a baseball player but a good guy to go along with it. The kind of guy you pull for.

I was lucky that I got to spend five years with him. He's the best double play man I've ever seen in my life. With the game on the line you'd hope they'd hit the ball to him because you knew it was an automatic out: Let's go home.

In five years with him, I never saw him make a bad throw to the shortstop on a double play ball, a ball that the guy had to get out of the dirt, or jump for, or move too much to one side or the other.

I watched this guy day in and day out and you'd just marvel at him. You'd just marvel at him! As a coach, what you'd do with him was leave him alone. We took many films of Maz, instructional films for other players, because how could you improve on what he was doing?

"We took many films of Maz"

He made double plays sometimes that you'd swear he couldn't turn...the guy running from first would be right on him, or there wasn't enough time for him to get rid of the ball but some way or another he managed to do it.

He had the greatest hands that a person could have. You just knew it was an out when they hit the ball to him. He made errors, of course, but I can't remember any of them. The reason I can't? He made errors in spots where it didn't hurt you. You wouldn't see him make an error when it's the last out of the game and we have a one-run lead and they've got a guy on third base.

The best way I can explain it: Bill was a baseball player. That's a compliment as far as I'm concerned. Because sometimes you can find guys that are playing baseball but they're not baseball players.

Bill came up in 1956. I had heard of him. You heard so much about how he could make the double play, what kind of hands he had. When you watched him, you weren't disappointed. Anything that was in his range was murder.

He made it look so easy on top of all that. He'd just giggle. You'd say something to him and he'd just laugh. I don't blame him. If I could play like that, I'd laugh too.

You'd go to spring training and it was just automatic that Maz is your second baseman. It's such an important position; when you get that kind of talent, you're fortunate.

Same way with the Tigers. I spent twelve years with the Tigers. When Alan Trammell and Lou Whitaker play short and second for you, you're not looking to make any changes – these are the kind of guys you pray to have. Once you get a guy like Maz, you stick with him till he drops. That's what they did in Pittsburgh; that's what they should have done.

Forbes Field was not the greatest infield by any means, but Maz never seemed to get the bad hop, because of the way he played the ball. You can create bad hops sometimes by the way you fail to attack a ball. On defense you have to attack the ball the same way you do on offense. As soon as the ball left the bat, Bill knew exactly what he wanted to do to avoid getting himself between hops, to avoid giving the ball an extra bounce. He was just an excellent, excellent infielder.

So good in fact that the Pirates were able to trade Julian Javier, a talent at second base, to get the pitcher they needed, Mizell, from St. Louis for the stretch drive in 1960 when they won the Series. That says a lot for Mazeroski.

Yes, I could catch the ball. But oh, when I first came up to the major leagues there were so many great infielders. Roy McMillan in Cincinnati had the most accurate arm you could possibly have. I always claimed that Roy McMillan could play shortstop with a blind first baseman! Just hold the glove up and he'd throw the ball in there. He was that accurate.

So many. Red Schoendienst. Red looked funny doing it sometimes but he never missed the ball. Great hands.

They've got some great ones today too. Ozzie Smith, he's done things that no other shortstop that ever played the game could do. The great ones always find a way. That's true with Bill. I think a lot of that has to be born in you. You can't just take a guy who's a so-so infielder and say all of a sudden I'm going to make a great infielder out of this guy. You can improve him through hard work though.

I was coaching at Cincinnati and Pete Rose was playing left field for us. We needed a third baseman. Sparky Anderson talked with Pete, I was standing there, and Sparky said, "I'll take you out for two or three days and hit you a lot of ground balls." Pete said, "You want me to play third?"

Sparky said, "Yeah, I'd like for you to try it." Pete said, "How about tonight?"

"How about tonight?"!! We went out and hit him some ground balls and Pete played third that very same night. Takes courage to do that.

Getting back to Maz, if there has ever been a case of leadership by example, it was Maz. He would never complain. You know, there are always little things you could gripe about and these things can be poisonous to a club if you get enough of them, creating dissension and disharmony. But you would never hear Maz complain.

Like the condition of the infield. Maz never worried about it. Other guys in the league, playing on an infield that wasn't so good, they'd be psyched out. Couldn't catch a ground ball!

Maz would think who his pitcher was, who the hitter was,

how this guy has hit before, all these things that you gain through experience.

It was such a good feeling to be on a team with a guy who you have so much confidence in that you never thought he would miss a ball or throw a ball away. And Bill Mazeroski would do something every day to help you win a ballgame, whether it be with a bat or with a glove.

*"**I** have always admired Bill and appreciated his ability, but even more than that, his friendliness, his humbleness."*

– Bobby Richardson

22

Bobby Richardson

Bobby Richardson was the starter at second base for the great New York Yankee teams that won five consecutive pennants, and two World Series, from 1960 through 1964. A fine fielder who earned five Gold Gloves (1961-1965), Richardson was a .266 lifetime hitter, reaching .300 twice and leading the American League with 209 hits in 1962. Richardson produced many record batting performances in the World Series. In 1960, Bobby drove in 12 runs (a record 6 in one game), and became the only *Sport* magazine World Series M.V.P. ever named from a losing team; the next year he had nine hits in a 5-game Series; and in 1964, he rapped out 13 hits. Bobby retired at 31 to devote himself to his family and interests including a run for Congress and work with the Fellowship of Christian Athletes. Retired from coaching baseball at Liberty University and the University of South Carolina, Bobby serves on the board of B.A.T., the Baseball Assistance Team, which helps those in the baseball family who are in need.

S tarting out with the Yankees I was up for about a month in '55 and sent back down to Denver, Triple A. I had two good years in Denver, rooming with Tony Kubek. We formed a good double play combination. I came back up at the end of '56, so 1957 was my first full year. The Yankees won the pennant every year from 1955 to 1964, except 1959. We lost the Series in '57 and won in '58, against Milwaukee. In '60, we lost to the Pirates, '61 beat Cincinnati, '62 beat San Francisco, '63 were swept by the Dodgers, '64 lost to the Cardinals. By this time, I started thinking about retiring. I had boys growing up.

It was hard to move my family from South Carolina to Florida for spring training and then to New York. Tony Kubek and I went to the Yankees and told them we were both going to retire. They asked us to at least play one more year and not break up the double play combination. The next year I would retire and Tony would play on for at least one more year. Tony got a pinched nerve, and the Mayo Clinic said he shouldn't play, as that might result in permanent paralysis. The Yankees called me and said Tony can't play, will you play one more year, 1966? The Yankees finished in last place that year. It was a very tough year, for me and for the ball club.

They did give me a "Day" in New York, and a five-year contract, one to play that last year, and four to be a scout on special assignment. That gave me a chance to decide what I wanted to do. I did play at a great time and I retired young; I had just turned 31. I don't think the fans understood, just as I don't think they understand Ryne Sandberg, the Cubs' second baseman walking away, especially in the middle of the season. My priorities were toward my family. It was a good decision for me.

Paul Dietzel asked me to be baseball coach at the University of South Carolina; the Yankees and the Mets came down and we played three innings against the Yankees, three innings against the Mets, then they played each other under the lights. That put our program on the map at the university. We drew about 10,000 people and we kept improving, finishing second in the nation in '75. We were 51-6; we lost to Texas in the final two games of the College World Series.

I had been to the White House, spoken at a worship service and some other things, and President Nixon had asked me to run for Congress, which I declined to do. Then Gerald Ford and I became friends and I resigned, after we finished second in the nation, to run for Congress here in South Carolina in 1976. I ran as a Republican in a state where seven of my ten counties didn't even have Republicans registered. It was a close race. Mantle and DiMaggio stumped for me; I lost the election by 3,000 votes out of 128,000 cast. My wife said I won, because I didn't have to move to Washington.

After a while I missed baseball, and became Athletic Director and baseball coach at Coastal Carolina, then I finished coaching at Liberty University and retired in 1990.

* * * * *

When Maz and I were coming along, it wasn't as organized, there were always a lot of pick-up games. Now you see Little Leaguers play that one year or two years, with the pressure some coaches put on them – I don't think they have as much fun as we did.

When I was 11, there would be a neighborhood game in my back yard or at the school grounds across the way. Those were my formative years for baseball.

I recall a guy I went with to most of the games who was about six years older. He'd played one year of minor league ball, and used to hit me ground balls; he recognized that I liked baseball and wanted to improve. He would hit fly balls to me in the outfield.

Let's talk about Maz. I have always admired Bill and appreciated his ability, but even more than that, his friendliness, his humbleness. In Oldtimers' games we don't take batting practice. All the others go up and see how far they can hit the ball and I don't ever swing the bat and he doesn't either. Maz has walked up there the first time and hit the first pitch out of the park for a home run. My reward in the '94 All-Star Old-Timers' game in Pittsburgh was having my three-year-old granddaughter standing behind the dugout, recognizing me in uniform for the first time, squealing, "Pop-Pop!"

I guess Maz plays a lot of golf. I play a little bit. I have a tournament named after me for F.C.A., the Fellowship of Christian Athletes, where we raise money, but I don't play as much as Maz does and I'm not as good. The F.C.A. is about sharing what the Lord means to you. I think being a Christian helped me to be a better father, a better husband and just naturally a better ball player. You can turn the other cheek and still be a competitor, trying to get the most out of your God-given ability. The Lord has been an integral part of my life throughout baseball. I've headed up Baseball Chapel for the last ten years.

Every team in baseball, major leagues and minor leagues, has a devotion in the clubhouse every Sunday. Gary Carter stepped in last year to take over my position as president. We're averaging about fifteen guys on every ball club.

Players today face financial decisions that we didn't have. Phil Rizzuto told me that two years ago in Detroit, he and Bobby Murcer were going out to the park, and for a change they rode out on the team bus; usually they took a cab. On the bus, twelve of the Yankees had laptop computers as well as cellular telephones. They were buying and selling stocks on the way to the ballpark. Rizzuto wondered how they can concentrate on baseball.

When did I first see Maz? It would have been Class A ball. I was with Binghamton, he was with Williamsport. I remember thinking, oh boy, he's really a good fielder. Then the more I saw him the more I realized he was going to be a really good ball player. My thought at that time was, he'll be in the big leagues before too long. Maz was just a young boy, I was too, but he had the makings of a major leaguer right from the very beginning. The next time I really remember seeing Maz was the '60 World Series.

We scored a lot of runs, we had a good ball club, but we lost that Series. The key to the Series was Casey Stengel not starting Whitey Ford in the first game. Whitey Ford was "The Chairman of the Board," and when you have a World Series opener, that's who you start. Yet Casey didn't pitch him until the third game of the Series. I never did understand that.

The best fielder on that '60 club was Clete Boyer. Clete was as good as they come. You stand up Clete Boyer and Brooks Robinson, I'd take Clete any day as a fielder. And Kubek was underrated, he made all the plays. He just didn't look smooth.

* * * * *

I realized that I really belonged in 1957 when the Yankees chose to trade Billy Martin. I had been playing some at short, some at third, in and out, back and forth. When they traded Billy to Kansas City, that meant, okay, it's yours. I really felt at home in '61, when Ralph Houk took over; he had been my manager in Denver. Ralph had been like a father to me over the years. I was able to relax then.

I came up as a shortstop, just as Maz did, and Casey Stengel was nice but said we've got Mr. Rizzuto here: you'd better find a new position. Casey assigned Jerry Coleman to the rookie camp to teach me; Jerry was one of the best at making double plays. His philosophy was get to the bag as quickly as possible. Move a step closer to the bag – not many hitters are

1960 World Series: Bobby Richardson waits for the first pitch of Game 7 from Vernon Law. Bill Mazeroski looks on from second base. The catcher is Smoky Burgess, the umpire, Bill Jackowski

going to hit it one foot the other way – and be stationary. Get to the bag, straddle the bag and then you can either go to the left, wherever the throw is, or if it's a close play or slow-hit ball you go across like Maz could do. I never had any trouble with the double play, I was always able to just get the ball and get it to first base.

I don't remember ever being hit except one time, the World Series in '61. Frank Robinson slid into second base and I had five stitches put in. The only two runners I worried about were Bob Allison, and Roger Maris – who had great speed and a come-up slide that was almost impossible to jump over, when he was with Kansas City and Cleveland.

The secret on the pivot is having a strong enough arm to get rid of the ball, then opening your body so if you do get hit, you can just fall on top of the runner or jump over him.

Maz always had a reputation among baserunners: they knew he got rid of the ball quickly, so they'd slide a little bit farther out, because Maz would turn it so quickly that they knew they had to get down, they didn't want to get hit. That's automatic. You catch the ball, you throw it and you assume they'll be out of the way. You're not really aiming for them. I never hit anybody.

Was coaching important at the major league level? Absolutely. The Yankees were unique. They had Frank Crosetti, probably the finest coach in all of baseball. I always appreciated him very much.

When I was twelve years old, the Yankees came through Columbia, South Carolina. They split their squad, A team, B team. I went over to watch them play and Frank Crosetti was the shortstop. I remember he made two good plays that day. Five years later I was working out with the Yankees and the thing I remember as I started out on the field was Frank saying, come over here a minute. What size shoe do you wear? Frank Crosetti gave me a brand-new pair of cleats. He said, those cleats, you need a better pair than that. We became friends. He was there my whole career.

Everybody with the Yankees knew exactly who the cut-off man was; back up the cut-off play, be sure to tell the shortstop if you were out behind him what the play is, because his back's turned. I think that all stemmed from Frank Crosetti, spring training, rookie camps and good coaching in the farm system.

Fielding plays that stick in my mind? Of course, the last out of the '62 World Series. It wasn't a double play but it was a line drive. McCovey hit the ball to me. Ralph Terry was pitching. Houk went out to see whether he wanted to walk McCovey and pitch to righthanded Orlando Cepeda. I walked over to second base. Mays was standing on the bag; Kubek was loitering. Tony was kind of quiet then, though now he's a broadcaster, but he looked at me and said, "I sure hope McCovey doesn't hit the ball to you." I said, "Why?" Tony said, "Well, you've already made two errors this Series, I'd hate to see you blow one right now." That's what I was thinking about when I went back to my position! McCovey hit the ball, I caught it, we were the World Champions.

Years later McCovey asked me if I had moved over a little bit. I was playing him to pull. I don't remember moving at all. I wouldn't lean, but I'd know every pitch. Naturally on the breaking ball, I would be ready to move to my left a little bit.

I would also, when there was a change-up, let Moose Skowron at first base know it was an off-speed pitch so he'd be ready for a ball down his way.

I do think fielding has been underrated by the average fan. Fans that really have a knowledge of baseball understand the importance of fielding. They know what the double play means. They know when a shortstop goes in the hole, backhands a ball and throws it to first base that it's not a hit, and how important that is, because so many games are won or lost by one run.

A good defense is as good of an offense as you can possibly have. I'm thinking of high school when I was not a good hitter. But I could make the team because I could field my position! I realized then that it was important in baseball to field well. I will say that Whitey Ford and our pitching staff would always alert the fans and media that, hey, we've got a good infield. It's because our infield is doing well that we're able to be a contender each year. I cannot remember any championship team I ever played on, at any level, that didn't have a fine defense.

These days at second base, I like Roberto Alomar; he can make all the plays. When I played, one guy in the American League stood out – Dick Green. Most people have never heard of him, Dick Green with Kansas City. I felt he was then the premier defensive second baseman in the American League. Maz has always been the best in the National League. I don't think there's any dispute there.

Offensively I batted ninth when Stengel was managing the Yankees; any time Don Larsen pitched, or Tommy Byrne, he'd bat him seventh and bat me ninth! It was embarrassing. Stengel would get on me because I didn't get many walks. I'd reply, "How can I get walks with Maris and Mantle and Yogi and Skowron? They're not going to put me on base. They'll make me hit my way on."

With the bat, my worst experience was in 1964: even though I set a record with 13 hits in the Series, I made the last out. Bob Gibson was pitching. I already had seven hits off Bob but I flied out to center field with Maris coming up behind me. In '63, Koufax made us all look silly. I batted second, Kubek struck out and Mantle struck out. Next time around, same thing. The third time up, struck out again. I walked by Mantle and he shook his head and said, there's no use for me to go up there. Then he struck out. So all three of us struck out three times in a row.

In '61, against Cincinnati, I set a record with nine hits in a five-game Series. Playing thirty consecutive Series games, a lot can happen. Good memories.

I remember that even before the '60 Series the Yankees knew Maz could hit the ball out of the park – he had power and you had better pitch carefully to him. And scouting Dick Groat – such a good contact man on the hit and run. Tony Kubek and I felt it might even be profitable if neither one of us covered second on the hit and run – that both of us just wait and play our positions! That happened one time and we came up with that alibi later when we got mixed up and nobody covered.

* * * * *

The thing I remember most about the Yankees did not take place on the field. World Series time, we'd have a meeting, I remember it like it was yesterday, Hank Bauer, Gene Woodling, veterans of the ball club, saying this guy was with us, let's give him a full share, somebody else was up 15 days, he needs some money, let's give him a half share. They were just so generous. Those years when we were winning there was indeed a team spirit, personalities mingled together for the goal of winning.

Having support at home when you're on the road all the time is essential too. I give my wife Betsy all the credit.

My son was born during baseball season. Betsy had the baby here in South Carolina. I flew home, saw my son, and went right back to Cleveland the next night. My wife was an integral part of my success and it took an effort on her part to pull everything together.

These days I'm on the board of B.A.T., the Baseball Assistance Team, which helps old ballplayers who have difficulties. Not only major leaguers, but the baseball family, folks that played in the minor leagues for a certain length of time, even personnel, not necessarily players. I've seen players involved with alcohol, or some other things, on their deathbed and B.A.T. would step in. Helping a widow without money to bury her husband, or somebody who had a leg amputated, but didn't have any visible means of support.

Bob Gibson, Ralph Branca, Joe Garagiola, Earl Wilson, Joe Black, Robin Roberts, and Warren Spahn are some of the former players who are active in helping individuals through B.A.T. It's a worthy cause; what we're doing is taking care of our own.

*"**O**ver 17 years, saving thousands of runs is like driving in thousands of runs. It's the same thing. So, what's the difference?"*

– Bill Mazeroski

23

Bill Mazeroski

Born September 5, 1936, in Wheeling, West Virginia, Bill Mazeroski is arguably the greatest fielder ever to play the game of professional baseball. He played second base for the Pittsburgh Pirates from 1956 to 1972. A seven-time All-Star, Maz won eight Gold Gloves, in 1958, 1960, 1961, and 1963-1967. His major league records include leading the league in chances per game ten times, in assists, nine times, in double plays, eight times. Mazeroski's career total of 1,706 double plays and single-season mark of 161 double plays are also major league records. His dramatic home run in the bottom of the ninth inning of Game 7 of the 1960 World Series propelled the Pirates to an upset win over the New York Yankees. Mazeroski was named the Sporting News Player of the Year in 1960 and won the Babe Ruth Award as the outstanding player in the 1960 World Series. Maz ranks #75 on *Total Baseball's* all-time player list, ahead of most Hall of Famers.

I remember just playing with a rubber ball, around the neighborhood. I was four or five years old then. You have to catch a rubber ball with two hands. I used two hands all my life and still teach catching the ball that way.

To get my first baseball glove, I dug an outhouse hole for my uncle Og. That's when I started to play. We lived back in the woods so we always had a field to play on. My Dad had played a lot and wanted me to play baseball.

We played quite a bit of catch. When Dad showed me how to hookslide, I tore a hole in my school jeans and my Mom went crazy! I was a Cleveland Indians fan. Where I was raised, we didn't have electricity — we had battery radios and sometimes we had to save the batteries just to listen to ball-games. I liked Jack Graney and Jimmy Dudley, the announcers. They kept the game interesting.

We were closer to Pittsburgh, living in the Upper Ohio Valley, in the southeastern part of Ohio. But I was faithful to Cleveland, the team from my home state. And in those days, Pittsburgh never won; Cleveland won the World Series in 1948 and the American League pennant in 1954. Some of my favorite players on the Indians were Lou Boudreau, Joe Gordon, Ken Keltner, Early Wynn, Bob Feller, Larry Doby, and Dale Mitchell.

I did play some second base before I went to high school. I played with a pick-up team that played other small-town teams around the area. My uncle Og coached that team. He was a good manager, the first one to put me at second base. I guess he knew what he was doing. I played shortstop and pitched in high school.

I broke in as a shortstop in the minor leagues. I played half a year and then went to spring training. They used to have young kids go two weeks early to spring training before the major leaguers got there. There were six to eight shortstops, so they put me at second in an intrasquad game. Some left-handed pull hitter hit a ball to the shortstop. I was playing way over. I ran over to second base, caught the ball and threw it to first, all in one motion. Branch Rickey saw that and said, "Leave that kid at second. He is now a second baseman." That's how I became a second baseman in professional ball.

Al Burazio, my high school coach, wanted me to play semi-pro and play in the coal miners' league with older men to get used to that. He felt when you go out and play for a living, you're going to be playing with older people. When I graduated from high school I was seventeen. I was sent to Class A ball, playing with guys who had been in the big leagues; some were on their way down, not quite good enough to stay there. If you're going to go anywhere, you have to improve, and I think I did. I probably missed something by not playing a little bit of American Legion, but in the long run playing with older players in semi-pro was good for me.

* * * * *

Growing up, if it was summertime, I had my glove with me everywhere I went. But when basketball season came, I was a basketball player, too. I played all through high school. I was All-State in basketball. Averaged twenty-eight points a game. When it was cold, I was shooting basketballs off the barn. We didn't have a very good team. I'd have to bring the ball up and then move inside and play the pivot. My Dad said no to football. I was upset at that, but it worked out for the best.

There was always a place to bounce a ball on a cement wall and catch it. We didn't have baseballs. I lived along the Ohio River — after a flood my sister, Mary Lou, and I would walk the river and look for balls, rubber balls, to play with. We'd find a few dozen and I'd wear them out, banging them up against the brick wall and catching them.

That's one reason my hands got quick. Those rubber balls really bounce when they hit stones and things, and that quickens your reflexes. That was a big part of my training. If I promised to do her chores, my sister would also pitch to me!

It was easier in those days. Not as much for kids to do. We didn't have cars — we were all stuck there, we'd congregate in one place and go play ball. It wasn't organized like now, but guys just went out and played, with more fun and enjoyment then. Sometimes in Little League kids get too much pressure put on them, they don't like the game, they quit sooner. I don't agree with parents yelling at their kids like I've seen a

Opposite page, from top:
A very young Maz;
with sister Mary Lou;
Bill as teenager

This page:
Bill's mother, Mayme;
Bill's father, Lew

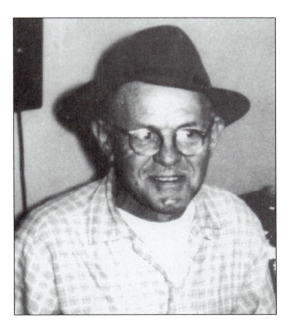

The star player for Warren Consolidated High School in Tiltonsville, Ohio crosses the plate

17-year-old high school graduate, 1954

lot of times. There shouldn't be any pressure for a kid to win or get a base hit when he's nine, ten years old. That's the time to have fun, not feel pressure.

I taught my son Darren how to play. I was trying to teach him when he was ten years old. I said, "Now, this is how you've got to do it." He'd work at it for fifty seconds, then he wanted to play. I didn't blame him. I told him, "When you're ready to get serious and learn, you let me know."

Above: Darren Mazeroski gets a pointer from his mother, Milene

Right: Darren suits up as Pirate catcher while Dad looks on

Three years later, as a freshman in high school, Darren came to me. He was ready to learn. Darren did a fine job in high school. He won a scholarship to college and played one year professionally.

Phil Niekro? He threw the knuckleball in high school in Ohio as a freshman, pitching in relief. The second time I saw him he started against me. I beat him for his only loss in high school.

I pitched a double-header the day of the Ohio State High School Championship Tournament. I won the first one and lost the second one, 2-1 or 2-0. I had better stuff the second game than I did the first.

Al Burazio, my high school coach, was there when I was growing up and learning the most. One thing about Al, he was as good at teaching the fundamentals as anybody I've been around.

Amateur and professional baseball. He was a good teacher of how to make contact, hitting the ball. And like I said, I still teach today how Al taught me to catch the ground ball, with two hands.

It helped to have that good instruction early. I practiced the right way all those years and didn't develop too many bad habits. I stayed with what proved to be a good way to catch the ball.

When I was a freshman, Burazio said, "I'll make you a big leaguer." I didn't think much of it. But it sounded good. I guess he knew what he was talking about. He never said that to anybody else.

It's just something you want to be. You listen to the Indians on the radio and, "Boy, would I like to be there doing that." You think about it all the time when you're playing — but you really don't know if you're good enough. You know you're better than guys you're playing with in high school. So you figure you're going to go a step further. With each step you take, you find out a little more about yourself. You have to keep improving.

In those days, kids didn't go to college to play baseball. If you wanted to play baseball, you signed and went to the minor leagues: Class D and C and B and A. Most kids went to

Class D out of high school. I was lucky. I went to Class A, Williamsport, Pennsylvania, the Eastern League, a pitcher's league. Those pitchers were better than the ones I had been facing. I hit .235 that year. I played shortstop, and wasn't very consistent at seventeen. I threw a lot of balls away.

How many games do you play in high school? If we got in nine or ten games in high school, we were lucky, with the weather we had. Maybe thirty, forty games a summer, in semi-pro — the miners' league and *Times-Leader* newspaper league. I never got as much playing time as I would have liked. But I started to improve that first year when I went to winter ball to play maybe fifty, sixty games. Then I'd come back and play all summer. I started to catch up with everybody else. I kept improving.

We were the pioneers, teams sending players over to the Dominican Republic. They had all been going to Puerto Rico, Cuba or Venezuela, but nobody went to the Dominican. This was the first year they had a league there with connections to major league teams. It was a little rough at first but everything got worked out. I still think playing winter ball was the most important time in my career. I enjoyed it.

I used to worry about making errors and people booing me, but over there I couldn't understand what they were saying, so it didn't matter. I just relaxed, got more confident, and learned how to play.

First year over there, I was a shortstop and I'm turning a double play. Ball's hit to the second baseman and I'm turning it real quick. They never saw that before. On the first day or two of practice, we'd draw a big crowd just to watch. I'd turn a double play and they'd yell. I mean, they'd just "oooh," they'd scream, they'd say, "Did you see that? Look, look, look, look." Everybody. Three or four hundred people there yelling. And I thought they were looking to see how far somebody hit a home run. They were standing up cheering me. A standing ovation in practice just turning a double play from shortstop! They had never seen anybody with quick hands and feet like that. It was really weird.

The second year in pro ball, I went to Triple A for a month with the Hollywood Stars and hit .170. I wasn't ready for

Triple A. Back to Williamsport I went. I hit .293 there. Had eleven home runs, drove in some runs; I was playing second base then.

Went to winter ball again in the Dominican league and did well. Went back to Hollywood in the Pacific Coast League, and played about half a year, hitting .320 when I heard I was coming up. Then I played three more games and went 0 for 12, I think. I was so excited about getting to the big leagues. I went down to .306 by the time I came up July 7th, 1956. I was 19 years old, gaining valuable experience.

The very first game up was in the Polo Grounds. Johnny Antonelli of the New York Giants was pitching. My first at-bat I hit a line drive in the seats. Just foul. Then I hit a chopper up the middle and beat it out for a base hit. My high school coach Al Burazio was in the stands that day, as he had promised.

With high school coach Al Burazio: "As good at teaching the fundamentals as anybody I've been around"

First month in the majors, July 1956

That first game I also turned my first double play. Willie Mays hit the ball to short and we doubled him up.

It was a dream come true to be there. That first year I hit .243.

The next year, 1957, I came back but I wasn't starting. Bobby Bragan was managing and he thought I was too young. Somebody sprained an ankle or wrist, and I got to play just as I was about to ask the General Manager to send me down so I could play every day somewhere. I kept playing, ended up hitting .283 and was in the big leagues for good. But it took somebody getting hurt for me to get another chance. Somebody else's bad luck was my good luck.

I was fortunate that I had played winter ball with some guys on the team. I was always the young kid. They took me under their wing and watched over me. When I came to Pittsburgh I felt pretty comfortable. I'd played as well as they had in winter ball, and I wasn't quite as nervous as if I'd just come up not knowing anybody.

* * * * *

Who did I like to watch? Roberto Clemente was a joy to watch and great to play with for seventeen years. Roberto was a great guy and a good friend. Hank Aaron. Willie Mays. Stan Musial. In the American League, Mickey Mantle and Ted Williams.

Sandy Koufax was the best pitcher of my era because he had the best fastball and the best curveball. Two great pitches. Most great pitchers have just one. I didn't enjoy hitting off of Sandy, but it was fun to watch him. Same with Juan Marichal. He came at you from all angles.

Fielders...Curt Flood, Roy McMillan, Brooks Robinson. Flood played center field; I mostly watched a lot of infielders to see if they did anything different. I'd pick their brain whenever I could; most would do the same with me.

Bobby Richardson, Nellie Fox, Luis Aparicio, I never got to know those American League guys very well because I never got to see them. After we retired, Bobby and I became good friends and played in Old-Timers' games together. But when we played I'd only see him maybe once or twice in spring training. And All-Star games. It's a thrill to play in an All-Star game.

I think the most nervous I ever was happened at an All-Star game. We were taking infield and we were about to turn the double play — the American League players stopped playing catch. They'd all heard about me turning the double play, I guess they wanted to see for themselves if I was that good. I could just see them out of the corner of my eye, all watching. I said, "Uh oh. What do I do now?" I never thought about making the double play, I just did it. Now I was thinking. For me that was dangerous. The double plays weren't my best. I didn't take any chances. But everything worked out. It was quite an honor, being picked seven times to play in All-Star games.

* * * * *

When I first came up, I was a pull hitter. An inside fastball hitter: that's the one pitch I could hit out of the ballpark. I would try to pull the outside pitch, and I'd hit a weak ground ball to shortstop.

264

Roberto Clemente: "A joy to watch and great to play with for seventeen years"

In 1957 the Pirates tried to teach me to hit to right field, and I would try that with the inside pitch and get jammed. That was not one of my good years. In 1958 though, I hit nineteen home runs, drove in sixty-eight runs and hit .275, a pretty good year in Forbes Field.

If I'd played in some other ballpark and hit the same balls, I think I'd have hit a few more than nineteen home runs that year. Now that may sound like a lot of talk but it's not, really. Forbes Field was 365 down the left field line, with a big high scoreboard, 406 dead left, and 430 left center. I hit fifteen other balls off the scoreboard for doubles that may well have been home runs in Greenberg Gardens [a fenced-in area that shortened left field to help Pirate slugger Hank Greenberg] or somewhere else. Your home ballpark has a lot to do with your statistics.

I hit .260 lifetime. I didn't think of it at the time, but over a season the difference between .260 and .300 is a hit a week. One lousy hit a week doesn't seem like much, but it's the difference.

December 1957, Fort Knox, Kentucky: An M-1 rifle is in good hands with Pvt. Mazeroski

We finished second in '58. We felt pretty good about coming back in '59 and having a shot at winning. We finished fourth. It all came together in '60 for us, but I don't know what happened in '59. That season Haddix's 12 perfect innings game was a joy to play in. He was perfect. It's different playing in a no-hitter. You don't want to be the one to mess it up, so that adds a little pressure. I loved it!

In the clubhouse, before the first game of the series, the pitcher goes over the hitters and tells how he's going to pitch them. Just about everybody says, "I'm going to pitch them low and in, high and away, or high and tight, low and away." Don Hoak said, "If you pitch them that way, you'll pitch a no-hitter, Haddix."

Everybody laughed and that broke up the meeting. Darned if he didn't. I mean, Harvey had the Braves just eating out of his hand. They didn't hit the ball hard at all. One of the greatest games ever. It was fascinating to watch. We just couldn't score. Men on third, I think, two or three times with less than two outs and we couldn't get a run in for Haddix. We never did score, but if we had scored, Harvey wouldn't have had to go twelve perfect innings and pitch the greatest game ever pitched. Lew Burdette wound up with a 12-hit shutout. He called Haddix after the game and told him, "You've got to learn how to spread your hits out."

In 1959 ElRoy Face went 18-1. When you have a year like that, you not only have to have ability, a lot of good things have to happen. That record will last a long time.

In 1960 we traded for "Vinegar Bend" Mizell, that extra pitcher we needed. He did a great job. I think we were five games ahead at the All-Star break, never in too much jeopardy. It was a great year. We had never won before. It's a feeling you never forget. Winning a World Series is the ultimate high in baseball.

The fielding on that club was good. Virdon in center, Clemente in right. Skinner in left, Hoak was good at third. Stuart wasn't the best at first, but Rocky Nelson was good. Groat always did a fine job at shortstop.

First game of the 1960 Series, the first time up, I struck out. The same pitch the next time up I hit for a 2-run homer.

Inside fastball from Jim Coates. We won the game and knew we could beat them. They were human. Then they come back and beat us 16-3! Got into our bullpen. Whenever they did that, we were hurting. Unless it was ElRoy — he saved three games.

We didn't score on Whitey Ford in two games. Haddix and Law came back and beat them, then the Yankees shut us out and score twelve runs. We just outscored them in the last game. That was a good Series. A lot of runs scored and some close games.

That seventh game had to be one of the most exciting games ever played. It had everything.

Taking the field for the final inning, we had a two-run lead. I figured all we'd do is go out there, get three outs and we're world champs. All of a sudden, boom, boom: they tie the game. Starting out as a Cleveland Indians fan, I was never fond of the Yankees, but I respected them. They'd find ways to beat you all the time. I thought, don't tell me they're going to do that to us now. I even forgot I was leading off. Somebody had to tell me, "You're up, Maz."

Leading off the bottom of the ninth against Ralph Terry, the score was 9-9, and I had no idea what he was throwing. First pitch was a high fastball. Terry keeps saying his second pitch was a slider, but if it was, it didn't slide. Everybody knew I was a high fastball hitter. The Yankee catcher, Johnny Blanchard, hollered at him, "Hey, get the ball down." Terry got it down, but it was still high.

I wasn't trying to hit a home run. I was just trying to hit the ball hard. When I hit it I didn't know if it was going out. It was 406 feet out there and a high wall. Yogi Berra was in left and I knew he wasn't going to catch it. So I wanted to be on third if he misplayed it off the wall. I was running hard all the way to first and going into second. Then I looked up, saw the umpire and heard the noise of the crowd. It struck me that the ball had gone out of the park, and I went crazy. It was over. We beat the Yankees.

I never touched ground from second to home. I just floated in. But I knew I had to touch home plate. That was no problem. When I got there my teammates formed a "V" and I had just enough room to get my foot in. Probably the first and only time I showed my emotions on the field.

As kids, we'd say, "It's bottom of the ninth, game tied..." With stones and a broomstick that you pick up — I remember doing that all the time. Hitting stones with a broomstick, pretending to be Babe Ruth or Joe DiMaggio. You'd pick out a spot: out there is a single, that spot's a double, triple, home run, you know. I got to live that dream. I am one of the lucky people in the world.

After the game everybody went Downtown to have a good time. My wife Milene and I went the other direction to Schenley Park. It was still daylight. We sat and relaxed. Not a soul up there. Just squirrels.

October 13, 1960: The most important home run in baseball history leaves Forbes Field. "I wasn't trying to hit a home run"

Heading for home and a welcoming committee of world champion Pirates

"Probably the first and only time I showed my emotions on the field"

*Above: Pirates manager Danny Murtaugh with the
1960 Babe Ruth Award winner as outstanding player
in the World Series*

*Opposite page, top: Murtaugh delights in the luck of
the Irish (and Polish); bottom: the bat that won the
1960 World Series, now on display in Cooperstown*

Later that night the team had a victory party at one of the hotels. A great time was had by all.

I couldn't let hitting that home run become too big. I still had twelve years to play and you don't live off of one hit. You've got to keep producing. I put the home run in the back of my mind and worked as hard as ever to stay in the big leagues.

* * * * *

In '61 things didn't go well. After the '62 season when we didn't win, the Pirates traded away the infield, except for me. Time for a change and here I was 26 years old, the old man of the club. I had had a pretty good year. I led the club in RBI's, with eighty-one. Hit low in the lineup, too. I didn't hit third or fourth or fifth. I hit seventh or eighth.

After the trades the Pirates wanted me to take more control and be a leader, so they gave me the captain's job. The captain gives the umpires the lineup before a game, and acts as a go-between for the players and the manager. I was captain after Dick Groat and before Willie Stargell.

Shortstops each do some things a little differently but if you practice enough together, you get used to each other. One's strong point may be another's weak point. Working together you iron all that out. It doesn't take too long.

Dick Groat was a student of the game. He played the hitters well, had good hands and an accurate arm. He was great at feeding me for the double play. He also hit .300 most of the time. Dick was a great hit-and-run man who hit to the opposite field with the best of them. A real team player and a winner.

Gene Alley was also a good shortstop with great range, a really strong arm, a soft touch and accurate feed. Gene hit .299 one year and was one of the best shortstops of his era. Gene and I got along very well together; he was my roommate and a good friend.

I don't think you can catch the ball and turn a quick double play. The ball has to ricochet from your glove to your bare hand. And your feet have to be ready before you get the ball.

Most people will catch it, set their feet, and then throw it, which takes extra time. You can't catch it and take a big step; at the same time you're taking that big step, the runner is covering twice that distance, so you're losing six or eight feet at first base if you do that.

Once before a game, Harry Walker had me come over and work with Joe Morgan, when Harry managed Houston. The Pirates were playing the Astros. Harry had me come out to the ballpark and work with Joe Morgan on how to turn the double play. Joe got better. That was unusual, an opposing player coming over and helping another guy on the other team.

Harry was the first one to show me, in slow-motion film of the double play, that I didn't touch the bag, I was off the bag. When I caught the ball and threw it, I was never on the bag. I could have sworn that I never cheated, but I cheated on every play. You couldn't see it with the naked eye, so how could you consider that cheating?

I loved the Forbes Field infield. A lot of people wouldn't even take ground balls on it. I liked it. I got used to it. It was hard all the time. At least it was consistent.

* * * * *

Some of the pitchers I wasn't happy about facing were Koufax, Bob Gibson, Marichal. Tom Seaver, Tony Cloninger, Jim Maloney used to throw hard.

It starts from the first pitch. You look for a pitch in your zone and the right speed. If you're looking for a breaking ball, that's fine. You're looking for a speed and a zone, so you can hit it and drive it hard somewhere.

Each strike after that, you tone it down, you're not as particular. Maybe if it's off of that zone a little bit and it's still in the hitting area, and I was not completely fooled, I'd swing at it. After two strikes, if it's close, you take your chances and whack.

Even though pitchers know the hitters, we know the pitchers. We know what they like to throw in certain situations. I was not a good curveball hitter, but I drove in a lot of runs when I would sit on the curveball. That's what they'd throw

"After two strikes, if it's close, you take your chances and whack"

when they were in trouble with a man on second or third and I was up. I'd get lots of breaking balls, and I just started looking for them and driving in runs.

But I didn't hit them when there wasn't anybody on, because I didn't concentrate that way. I couldn't concentrate at the plate in a 10-0 game or a 12-2 game. Concentrate and get that extra hit. Maybe that's where I could have gotten that one extra hit a week.

* * * * *

Roommates...life on the road wasn't bad when you're young, single. You don't mind being away from home. It's fun. My first roommate was Red Munger, an old right-handed pitcher who chewed. Chewing in the room, spitting in the garbage can. Uggh. How could a guy do that? I'd never chewed or anything and I couldn't believe anybody would do that. Later on I started to chew, and I chewed most of my career, but I quit years ago.

"Vinegar Bend" Mizell also roomed with me. Bill Virdon and Gene Alley, I think, were the longest. Virdon for four or five years and Gene Alley for four or five years. Both quiet. Then Steve Blass for a year or so.

I'd prefer a roommate to nowadays where everybody pretty much rooms alone. At least you had somebody to talk to, go to breakfast with, or have a drink with after the game. Baseball was the main subject, talking about other players. "What would you do here?" "Why would he do that?" Unless we got into football or other sports. We weren't smart enough to talk about too many other things, I guess.

* * * * *

1966, the year we went right down to the wire. That year, I had a hundred and sixty-one double plays. The team set a league record with two hundred and fifteen. You never thought much about it until after the season was over. Then you look back and try to figure which one you missed. I might have thrown one away at first, and Gene might have let a ground ball go through his legs one day. We might have missed two, possibly three double plays that year. Pretty good, but still room for a little improvement.

I played seventeen years at second base. Nobody ever took me out at second. On the double play, I got kicked a lot and bruised a lot, but I never missed any innings of ballgames because of it. A dozen or so runners never showed up the next inning; two or three were carried off, couldn't show up for a while. They slid into these ol' stumps here; I had them anchored and they didn't give.

When you throw, your knee is bent, your toe is facing first base, and all your weight is forward while releasing the ball. On a close double play, when the runner slides into your knee and shin, it's just like hitting a tree stump. It doesn't move. The spikes are dug in the ground. You don't get hurt as long as your toes are facing the runner. However if you get caught sideways, your knee could get caved in. As a rule, runners don't try to spike you, but they do try to turn you inside out.

Turning the double play, I never looked at the baserunner. I

just looked at first. He's in the way, too bad. I never hit anybody, I don't think. I came awful close.

You get a reputation that you're not afraid. Just like when
Vada Pinson was a rookie on the Reds — veterans used to
tempt every rookie: "There's a hundred dollars if you can take
Mazeroski out at second." So Pinson comes down to second,
he's going to earn that hundred dollars, and he slides into my
knee and comes limping off the field. The Reds were all
laughing at him in their dugout. That was the last time Vada
came close to me. To this day when I see Vada he still talks
about that slide and the hurt.

I broke my foot in 1965. I was running the bases and tried
to stop in the hard dirt. Out about six weeks, an awfully long
time to be out. Watching games from the stands wasn't much
fun at all.

While I was out I learned how to play golf. I got Ben Hogan's
book and went step by step. I had a cast from the knee down
but I could walk. I learned how to play golf from scratch. Got

*"Like hitting a tree stump": San Francisco's Matty Alou is called out at
second by umpire Tom Gorman*

some plastic balls down in Florida and just hit them into the wind. By following Hogan's instructions, I've been able to shoot in the low 80's and high 70's. Well, most of the time.

Yes, one year I played one hundred and sixty-three games. I think about three or four years in a row, I played a hundred and sixty or so. I got up to 392 games in a row, from August '65 through May '68. That was a league record for second basemen at the time.

I played every day, because whether I was hitting or not, I thought I could help win the game defensively. And the pitchers wanted me in there, because they wanted the double play. Pitchers rely on defense and the double play is their best friend. They didn't care what I hit.

At times throughout a year I would get tired, my bat would get heavy. I'd go 0 for 25 or 30, a long stretch without getting any hits. I played through it and wouldn't take any days off to get some rest. I think a couple of days off could have helped my batting average, but I was helping the team, and my average didn't matter to me.

You can't play seventeen years for the same team if defense is all you have. It doesn't matter how good your glove is, if you don't get hits, you won't be a starter in the big leagues for very long. I didn't consider myself strictly a defensive player. You don't get 2016 hits and drive in 853 runs if you're a defensive player only.

* * * * *

1971. Steve Blass, Manny Sanguillen, Richie Hebner, Al Oliver, Bob Robertson, most came up within a year or so of each other. We knew they could play a little bit. Gene Alley was a good shortstop when healthy. Dave Giusti came over from St. Louis and became a good relief pitcher.

Nellie Briles came over, too. And Bruce Kison. Willie Stargell had come up a little bit earlier, in '63. You knew he was going to be a good one. Clemente was still there. Pretty good ball club.

In the 1971 World Series Baltimore beat us the first two games in Baltimore. Then we beat them three in a row. We played in

Toasting a 1971 League Championship Series triumph over San Francisco, with the help of Willie Stargell

the first night World Series game that year. Bruce Kison pitched that evening. And then Briles pitched a great Game 5. We lost the sixth game, then Blass won it 2-1 in the seventh game.

I didn't play. I think I pinch-hit once in that Series, the first game, and that was it.

The last two seasons, I knew the end was getting close, because every time I did something, stretching for a ball, I'd pull a muscle. With these legs as big as they are — and I was starting to put on a little more weight. It was time. I was thirty-six when I quit.

Nowadays, they play up until they're forty. But with this body, you couldn't. With these legs, tight and big, every time you stretch them, they would pop and when I got in shape, it would stretch my back and I'd get a sore back. There was no use fooling yourself. It was over.

Error, spring training 1971: "The last two seasons I knew the end was getting close"

I was confused about whether I wanted to coach or not. A sportswriter friend, Chuck Feeney, said, "Maz, coach a year and see if you like it, then when you quit, you won't be quitting as a player, you'll be quitting as a coach."

I took Chuck's advice, coached a year and found out I did not like it that well. Same travel, doing twice as much, getting to the ballpark much earlier, leaving a little bit later. Taking care of twenty-six guys instead of one. Meanwhile my sons are growing up. They're young, they need me, so I decided to quit after the first year of coaching.

I didn't have the makeup for managing either. Danny Murtaugh was a good manager. He did a good job. The only thing I had against Murtaugh was he introduced me to my wife. Just kidding. He had played second for the Pirates back when I was a Cleveland fan. I was a kid who never knew much about baseball, just what I heard through the Cleveland radio station. We never got a newspaper.

I had some good managers. Bobby Bragan, Murtaugh, Harry Walker, and Bill Virdon; Bill was there my last year. I also coached third for Bill in 1973.

I'm not outgoing. Managers have to be firm and I'm not the firm type. You have to get up and talk to the Kiwanis. I hate that. I don't like to be in the public eye, the center of attention.

I didn't like coaching that much. I coached in Seattle in 1979 and 1980. The town and the kids were great, but I couldn't get home to see my family or friends; everything was a major road trip, and the American League never gets to Pittsburgh. In 1979 Seattle had never had a winner. A pretty day was your worst day at the ballpark, because fans went to the beach or boating. When it rained, they might come to the Kingdome. A little different.

Advising Richie Hebner to stay on third, 1973: "I didn't like coaching that much"

I was out of baseball for a few years until Virdon managed at Montreal. I went to spring training and worked with their infielders. I think I helped third baseman Tim Wallach a little. At least he said I did.

Players in my day used to go out and talk to fans. I don't think fans today get to meet or appreciate players like they did in the old days. No close-knitness to the community. Players today are not with one team long enough to get to know the fans.

It's more individualism than anything else. That's what everybody writes about. You get publicity for what you do, not for what your team does. To be complete, you have to win, and you need a team to do that.

Why bunt? There's no money in bunting. Why learn how? "Hey, if I have to bunt, I'll try." But you'd think if you had to bunt to win a game, you'd know how to bunt. Everybody in our day knew how to bunt: Clemente was a good bunter, Stargell, Aaron, and Mays could all bunt. They all practiced it. Didn't bunt all the time, but they knew how to do it.

You've got twenty-eight teams now. When I came up, we had sixteen teams. Just think if you had only two eight-team leagues, putting the best of today's teams together, what better brand of ball you would have, how competitive would that be! Four or five players on each team now shouldn't even be in the big leagues. Give these players time to learn the game down in the minor leagues; they'll be more experienced when they come up.

* * * * *

Brushback pitches...today pitchers are reluctant to pitch inside. If they come too close, somebody comes charging the mound. That used to happen only against pitchers who did it all the time. But if a guy hit a home run in front of you, as the next guy you automatically went down. You might as well go up there and lie down. Next time you come up, if you'd hit a pitcher hard up the middle or a line drive past him, boom, down you go. You expected it. You didn't charge the mound. Dig in deeper and try to hit it harder.

A lot of guys in those days wouldn't be allowed to pitch today. Like Bob Gibson. He'd fight every game because he pitched inside. He thought the inside part of the plate was his and you weren't allowed to touch it. Don Drysdale knocked a ton of people down. They called Sal Maglie "The Barber." He threw close to your chin all the time.

I never had any problems with any umpires. One time in San Francisco — Dascoli was the umpire's name. Seemed like a grouchy umpire. I caught the ball with a runner coming from first, I was playing in, made a swipe and it looked like I hit him. But to me, it didn't feel like I touched him. Dascoli called him safe. Murtaugh comes running out there, charging out at Dascoli, chomping at the bit, starting to scream. "Did you touch him, Maz?" I said, "No." Murtaugh turned right around and went to the dugout. That umpire thought I was the greatest thing in the world. Dascoli said, "Most people don't ever tell the truth out here." So I got in good graces with the umpires. It got around the league that I was honest.

Now the neighborhood play, not staying around second base on the pivot...I don't know how some of those guys got away with that. I didn't do that. You can't make the double play from anywhere but close to the bag, if you want to make it quick.

If you stay around the bag, umpires won't mess with you. But when you cheat away from the bag, every once in a while, they'll call it. Men on first and third, one out and you try that, that's when umpires call it, when it hurts the most. So I just stayed around the bag. I've never been called for missing the bag or cheating.

Base-stealers? Maury Wills and Lou Brock were the two big ones. Willie Davis had better speed but lacked the quickness Wills had. Davis was probably the fastest guy I've ever seen in baseball.

On a steal, it depends on who's hitting, whether the shortstop is covering or the second baseman is covering. The signal was just open mouth, close mouth. That's all. If the shortstop opened his mouth, that meant I had it. If he kept it closed, then he had it. As soon as the runner takes off, you've got to take off, unless you cheat.

Which I used to do a lot on a hit and run, cheat towards second base: then I could wait, even see the runner take off, and I wouldn't have to leave until the ball's past the hitter because I've cheated a little bit. This way I had more range at second. But if I was playing here [normal second base] and the runner takes off — now I've got to take off when he does, to be able to get to the bag in time for the throw from the catcher. So, I'm taking off and now the hitter hits the ball where I was standing; I can't get it. But if I'm standing here [closer to second base], where I don't have to break when the runner breaks, the batter hits the ball, I go over and catch it. So, see, I'd pick up that much room, because I cheated over this way to cover more ground in the hole. It doesn't seem to make sense, but it's true.

I think I was better going to my left. Probably most infielders are because it's natural. You can reach and still see the field of play. Backhand is different, not as natural as going to your left. But I liked the backhand.

Avoiding bad hops...you charge the ball and pick the hop you want if you can. Stop and play the short hop or the big hop. There's a range that you can choose from with one stride that can usually take the in-between hop out of it. You want to catch it on the short hop or the long hop. You don't want that in-between hop. That's hard to teach. When the ball's hit, you don't have much time. You don't want to get caught on your heels.

I got hit in the mouth. I got hit in the jaw. Once in Pittsburgh. Once in St. Louis. I wanted to catch the ball over my right shoulder, just barely off center, on the side I'm throwing from, so I could get rid of it quickly. Also if it took a bad hop it went over my shoulder and not in my face. A lot of infielders catch the ball with only the glove. The ball hits, it can spin out. I showed Tim Wallach how to use two hands. He liked it and used it very well.

If you've seen me play, you've very rarely seen me double-clutch, groping for the ball in the glove. That's because I never caught the ball: it more or less ricocheted into my bare hand.

Catching the ball, then taking it out of the glove, slows you down. I had a small glove that had a certain kind of heel, no heel almost. Your glove has to become a part of you. When I closed it, I wanted the ball to stick there — that's why I took most of the heel padding out. You use every little advantage you can, catching that little thing.

I'd save my gamer for about four or five years. Since it would take two years to break one in, I was always breaking a new glove in. I had a gamer I played with only in games, never in practice; one glove sitting aside; one breaking in all the time.

I used an Early Wynn A2054 model all the way through. When I came up to the major leagues, I was using an old glove with wire on it, held together with shoestring. Sam Narron, the Pirate catcher's coach, called the Wilson people: "Can't you get this kid a glove?" One of our infielders was using that

"I had a small glove...your glove has to become part of you"

A2054. Even though it had a pitcher's name on it, that was the only glove I ever used.

I never spit on my glove, never put oils on it. The lacing never failed me. The shoemaker near Forbes Field knew my gloves quite well, sewing, gluing, patching.

I lost my gamer after the 1960 World Series. Next spring training, I'm using my second glove, and Clemente shows up with my gamer. It had been put in his bag after the Series by mistake. Roberto told me he'd tried to give that old glove away in Puerto Rico. None of the kids would take it.

I sent one of my gloves to the Hall of Fame. They wanted one. They've got my bat, my glove, a picture. I feel like I'm a part of it.

Defense is highly underrated by some fans and some sports-writers who have no idea what it's about. The best defensive teams with good pitching and a little bit of offense win; if you don't have defense, you can't beat anybody. Give them only three outs and you can play anybody. Don't give them any-thing. No errors, no walks, no stupid plays. Make them beat you.

We had great hitting teams in Pittsburgh and didn't win. Cincinnati had a team that hit 200-some home runs. They didn't win a pennant. There were a lot of teams with a good offense but not much defense that didn't win.

Whose fielding did I admire? I liked Brooks Robinson. He was fantastic. He wasn't super fast. Very quick for the first step or two, which is all he needed to be. And very good hands. He didn't have a great arm, but he had a quick arm and quick feet: he caught the ball and threw it right away. He did everything well. Did a great, great, great job. He was amazing. Mike Schmidt was mostly a power man. He was all right out there, though he wasn't any Brooks Robinson. Not many were.

Shortstop...Ozzie Smith seems to be one of the best. Ozzie has been great a long time. Mark Belanger did a good job. So did Dave Concepcion, as well as Groat and Alley.

At second...Kenny Hubbs was good with the Cubs. I don't remember him real well because he wasn't around a long time. He died in an airplane crash. Hubbs made all the plays.

Charlie Neal was a thin, rangy type with the Dodgers. Had good range and good hands, turned a double play pretty well.

First base — Wes Parker was real good. He was smooth over there. Bill White was a good first baseman.

One important play that involves all infielders, pitchers, and catchers is the rundown. You don't run behind the runner, you get off to the side where you can throw around the runner. We had one or two rundowns a week, maybe. It's hard to say who was the most elusive baserunner, because you don't see everybody caught in rundowns, to judge who does well and who's lousy.

Usually, the quicker guys like Willie Mays would be tough. There are certain things you do in rundowns that runners know about, because they see them practiced in spring training, when outfielders are being run down by the infielders. If I let the ball loose and I'm in right behind you, you stop quick and then, boom, I touch you, that's interference. Your good baserunners look for that.

Outfield...Clemente was great out there. I guess Al Kaline was too, over in the American League. Carl Furillo had a great arm. I saw him a couple of years when I first came up. Aaron played right field well. He could chase it down and catch it. He didn't make many mistakes, he'd hit the cutoff man. He was a darn good player, one of the best, along with Mays.

But I think Curt Flood, all in all, was a better fielder than Willie, not for throwing or anything, but just going and flat out catching the ball. But he didn't get the publicity Mays got. Flood just went out and caught the ball. My roommate Bill Virdon was very good out there, too.

Left field. Stargell had a good arm — almost as good as Clemente's. I knew when I first saw Stargell that he was going to be something special. When he hit the ball the sound was different from most hitters making contact. Carl Yastrzemski, there's a good one. I saw Ted Williams only in spring training a couple of times.

Clemente was one of the outfielders who didn't have to hit the cutoff man most of the time. Because he had such a strong arm, he could get it there on his own. When he was throwing to third, his throw was low enough to hit the cutoff

Holding the Cardinals' Phil Gagliano to a double: "Defense is highly underrated"

and still get to third in the air. Coming home sometimes, he'd miss the cutoff man and try to get it all the way to the plate. That's a lot longer throw than to third. Didn't hurt him because he got it there quicker than most people. Roberto was one of the very few right fielders who could field the ball with the runner rounding first and throw behind that runner, without him taking second. He threw out quite a few guys doing that.

I wasn't much of a base stealer. I was never on my own. Most of my steals came on hit and runs where the ball was missed or taken by the batter. I stole home once on a squeeze play when the ball got away from the catcher!

* * * * *

My reasoning for all the home runs now? Pitching is not as strong as it was when we had an eight-team league. All the expansion has thinned it out, and hitters are taking advantage. In our day, lots of guys threw 95, 96, 97 mph. Cloninger, Maloney, Sam McDowell, Bob Veale, Herb Score, Koufax. Just about every team had a guy who could throw that hard. You don't find that nowadays.

Pirates' pitchers...Bob Friend hardly ever missed a turn. He'd pitch over two hundred innings every year. Won twenty-two in '58. Vernon Law didn't have the sinker that Friend had. Law had good control. Knew how to pitch.

Vern wouldn't throw at anybody. Vern was a deacon in the Mormon church. He'd say, "Let's see how close I can come to him." There was a difference in his mind. If I throw at you and hit you, then I'm going to feel bad, but if I'm seeing how close I can come, then I just misjudged that a little.

Murtaugh once told Vern to knock this hitter down. Vern said, "Skip, it's against my religion. The Bible says turn the other cheek." Murtaugh replied, "It will cost you $500 if you don't knock him down." Vern paused a little while, then said, "The Bible also says an eye for an eye."

ElRoy Face had a great forkball. He got by with that for quite a few years. He threw just hard enough so you couldn't sit on his forkball and still hit his fastball. Then he would throw a little breaking ball, a little slider. And he did a great job, had a great career. I don't remember anybody else who threw the forkball while I was playing. Then Bruce Sutter and a few others came along. Now it's a big-time pitch. ElRoy had a cocky stride. He knew he was going to do the job. There was a feeling of confidence when he walked in. Roy belongs in the Hall of Fame. He was the finest relief pitcher in my era.

Bob Veale threw about as hard as any pitcher. If anybody threw a hundred miles an hour, Veale at times came close. When Bob had it all going, he could beat anybody. He had a good slider. He struck out sixteen Phillies one night. He could throw. Bob was in the class of McDowell and Score.

Harvey Haddix won quite a few. He did a good job. Control, and knowing how to pitch. Knowing hitters.

Dock Ellis was a Pirate pitcher who changed the whole thing. He was different. Didn't want to sleep in the same hotel, wanted his water bed, put his hair up in curlers, and I guess he did a few other things that have been publicized. He was one of the first I'd seen of the new breed.

Veale was the only strikeout pitcher we ever had who could strike somebody out with three fastballs. All the other guys had to be pitchers...they wouldn't overpower you, they would pitch to your weakness and use control.

Bob Moose was a sinkerballer. He'd make you hit it on the ground. Steve Blass was a slider and fastball pitcher. You'd hit more fly balls off of him. Giusti's big pitch was the palm ball...pretty good fastball, decent slider. But his palm ball was his out pitch. Moose's sinkerball was his out pitch. Bruce Kison, sinkerball, slider. He wasn't afraid to hit you or throw inside to keep you honest.

* * * * *

A nervous time for me was waiting for Opening Day. That was something special. You'd get a few butterflies. After Opening Day, get ready and go get 'em.

In the old days, we got close to newspaper guys; they traveled with us. Two or three writers, and two broadcasters. If you won or lost and did something, they'd come in. Four or five people around you asking you what you thought.

Now, you do something, you've got crowds of people around you. I don't think I'd enjoy that. Everybody wants to find out something personal, something that will sell papers.

When you were at the park, everything was on the record. You'd go have a drink and dinner with reporters, which we

Taking a breather during spring training

used to do all the time, sit and talk about baseball. They'd say, "Now, wait a minute. Is this on the record?" And you'd say, "No, this is not on the record." All right. And they'd respect that. It was easy in those days, a simple life. Not today. You can't trust anybody. Somebody might be writing a book! Anything you say or do, they'll put in the book.

Typical road trip? Go to Philadelphia, go to New York — then run down to Atlanta or somewhere like that. Usually nine- or ten-day trips. You'd go to three cities. Go to L.A., San Diego, and San Francisco. Long trip, maybe you'd hit Houston and St. Louis, or Chicago and St. Louis.

I might have taken two trains, New York to Philadelphia, maybe Philadelphia to New York. But if we didn't take trains from there, Philadelphia to New York, we took a bus because it wasn't that far. It was three hours. It'd take you an hour to get to the airport — longer to go by air than it would by bus or train. Just small airplanes then — we flew ten hours to get to the coast. They'd stop for gas here or there.

You lived out of your suitcase. You'd open your big Priesmeyer suitcase, with your three jackets hanging in it, had your shorts and shirts here, put the dirty clothes over in this area, pack it up and go to the next town. Open it up again. We didn't hang anything up in closets.

Same thing every trip. Just bring them home, get them clean, and have them ready to go again. Don't wear them at home. Just on the road. You had one set of clothes for the road.

Little intangibles can change the whole complexion of the game. Most people don't even notice. "How deep should I play with a man on second?" "Should I cover the hole this way or that way?" "Will he be trying to pull this ball?" "Has he pulled this pitcher other times?"

All this is going through your mind. "Well, Clemente has got the better arm. I'm going to shave the middle because Virdon's got the longer throw, not as good an arm. Maybe if the batter hits it hard in the hole here, the runner can score, so I'll move over here and I'll give him that base hit and take the one away here." Things like that go through your mind all the time. "How fast does this guy on second run, and where is he going to be when I catch it, if I have to go over here?" "If it's hit slow, what's he going to do and how fast is he going?" Line drive — you've got to know everything before it happens. You've got to play it out in your mind before it even happens. So you're not surprised when it happens. You've been through it already. These little things, which people who never played don't even think enter into the game, are important. Yet those guys know everything when you hear them talk.

The bare hand? I hardly ever used my bare hand. I was a two-handed fielder. Maybe if the ball had stopped — depending on how far away it was. At third base, I think they use the bare hand too much. Too much room for error there. They can come down and get it two-handed. I've seen Brooks Robinson do it a lot of times. When you do have to use one hand, I recommend using the glove hand.

We did have a couple of improvised plays when Gene Alley was at short. On a ground ball up the middle I'd be running

1956

1968

1970

1972

hard, reach out and backhand it, then flip it to Alley coming across; then he'd throw it to first. The first two times we made that play, the first baseman dropped the ball. He was surprised to see it come from Alley.

I've seen the hidden ball trick happen a few times, but not too often. It has happened. I never did anything like that. I'm boring.

The *Odd Couple* movie? They wanted Clemente to hit into a triple play. He didn't want to. They were going to give every-body participating one hundred dollars. The money did not matter. Roberto thought it wouldn't look good to hit into a triple play.

I was happy to hit into the triple play. I didn't care. I'd never been in a movie before. It didn't take long. Had the bases loaded and the other team's infield out there, with a pitcher. The first pitch, we wanted a line drive to the third baseman, and I hit one, over his head. He couldn't reach it. The next pitch, I hit a one-hopper and boom, boom. He touched third, threw to second, on to first. Two takes, it's over. I knew the pitcher would throw a fastball, which you can hit where you want — if you know it's coming. I told him where I wanted it: inside. Jack Fisher was the pitcher. He was saying, "Don't you hit this out!" I had hit a grand slam off of him earlier that year. The scene was filmed in Shea Stadium in New York. The whole Pirates team was invited to the *Odd Couple* premiere in Pittsburgh. There was a standing ovation in that joint when I hit into the triple play!

I liked Chicago. That was nice to hit in. All day games, too. And I liked the Coliseum in L.A. I think I hit eight home runs out of there one year. You'd just reach out and hit the ball into the left field fence or over it. I'd like to have hit there all my career. Just a nice fly ball to left field is a home run.

Candlestick Park is the worst place in the world to play. I hated it. Cold, windy, tough to catch fly balls. The wind even affects the high hopper. Blows it down or sideways. That fog comes in over that hill, you can see everybody huddled in the stands like it's the dead of winter. Papers flying everywhere.

The little pop-up behind me, if I knew it had a chance to drop, I used to just turn around and run for the spot. You give a quick look, you see it, you turn around and bust your butt and get back to that spot and turn around. The ball should be there. Those are the toughies. If the ball is dead in the sun, you can't see it. But flip-up shades would help if the ball was off the edge of the sun. If you look at it without glasses, you can't keep your eyes open, so you have no way of catching it. But at least with sunglasses on, you can keep your eyes open looking into the sun, locate the ball as soon as it drifts out of the sun, and catch it.

Communicating with any outfielder, his word is boss. Whenever he says something, you stop. If you're parked under the ball waiting for it, if he hollers, get out of the way. That's the rule of baseball. The outfielder takes charge of everything. If he says nothing and I keep going and run into him, it's his fault. It's a tough play, there is one little spot out there where he's not sure he can get to it, he's not sure you can get to it, and if he calls for it at the last minute, there's a problem.

Fielding on Astroturf is so much easier than fielding on dirt; you shouldn't miss any balls. At second base I made eight errors total one year; and my home games were played in Forbes Field. That's not short-arming anything, either. That's going after everything, as hard as you can.

I never believed in short-arming or trying to save an error by not getting in front of the ball, by backhanding it. If you miss it when you're in front of it, it's an error. But if you miss it backhanding it, they'll score it a hit most of the time. I never believed in doing that, but a lot of infielders do. They protect themselves that way. If I were the scorekeeper, I'd give them errors.

I know a guy who won a Gold Glove at first base. He didn't move very far either way. If it wasn't right at him, he didn't try for it, because he couldn't move. But he got a Gold Glove because he made the fewest errors. Who would you rather have? A guy making ten errors and catching a hundred and fifty more balls or a guy with two errors who caught a hundred and fifty less. I don't know how you give a Gold Glove to a guy who just stood there.

I still don't think there's anybody who played who could

catch the ball any better than I could, and I know there's nobody who could turn a double play any quicker than I could. The numbers prove I was the best in baseball at turning the double play. There haven't been too many people anywhere who can say they're the best at what they did.

Just catching a ground ball, I think I could catch it with anybody who played in any era. Just fundamentally catching the ground ball...I do believe that I was as good as anybody.

* * * * *

I got over two thousand hits while playing a position that takes skill. You've got to have some skill to really do the job at short and second. The positions that take the most defensive skill are catcher, shortstop, second base, then center field. Winning teams are strong up the middle. At catcher, Johnny Bench was as good as anyone who ever played. Manny Sanguillen did a good job for us. He had some great years with the Pirates.

Pitchers can help themselves fielding. But pitchers are different. We always accused pitchers of not being athletes. Of course, there are some. A lot, in fact. Vernon Law was good, Harvey Haddix was excellent. Harvey Haddix won a few Gold Gloves for his defense. Law was a good athlete, as was ElRoy Face. Later on, Dave Giusti and Steve Blass played their position well.

Working on relays is part of spring training. Getting in position, where to line up, different situations on the field, first and third, second and third, man on first, keep the guy from going to third. Good relays keep runners from taking extra bases. Saving bases is important. Keep that double play in order.

Every cutoff man has to have a backup in case of the overthrow or the short hop. And if it's a short hop, he's supposed to let it go so it's a good hop to the guy backing him up; then you don't kick it around. All you're doing is trying to prevent the extra base.

* * * * *

My first home run was off of Robin Roberts, a fastball high and in. Philadelphia's old Connie Mack Stadium. Robin was just trying to throw a fastball by me.

Peeking? Harry Walker used to like to do that. I did it one time, in Philadelphia, and hit a double. I peeked down there and I saw that catcher move over on the inside and I knew it was a fastball inside. I forget the Phillies' pitcher; he threw something inside, off the plate but hard, and I hit a rope down the line for a double. But that was too scary. If the catcher moves outside and the pitcher busts one inside, I'd be leaning out over the plate and I'd get killed. No more peeking for me!

With fielding, some things never change. Ground ball to third, the fielder bobbles it a little, tries to pick it up and throw him out. He knows he should stick it in his pocket yet he'll still throw it. He thinks, "I've got a chance if I make that perfect throw and get rid of it quick." Then he usually throws it away. It takes experience, and knowing your runners, deciding when to throw and when not to.

I see more and more that infielders don't get set to throw the ball. They do it on the run more often. Ozzie Smith probably started that trend — but he can do it. I'd still like to see most of them stop, set and throw instead of throwing on the run. Kids in college try to do that and they throw it everywhere. They see big leaguers doing it. But there are times you have to throw on the run.

But if you've got time, set and throw. Especially third basemen: they come in and field a little three-hopper and keep running, give it the sidearm throw off balance while they're moving. I say square up, catch it, and gun him out. Throw a strike over there with something on it!

I remember my favorite fielding play, against the Mets. Two outs and Tommie Agee on second. Ground ball deep in the hole; I had to really reach to my left, running on the outfield grass. I caught the ball and knew I couldn't get the guy at first.

I had thought ahead of time that on a hit, Agee would not stop at third, so after I turned all the way around, I threw to home. The fans thought I'd meant to throw to first: they yelled "Oh, No" because they thought I'd thrown the ball away.

That ball went right to Sanguillen on two hops. Agee was out at home by ten feet. All because the play was thought out before the ball was ever hit.

* * * * *

Contracts were unpleasant. No agents then — they'd send you a contract, if you like it, you sign it; if you don't, you go in and talk about it or write a letter. I always went in and talked, got it over with. It was like a root canal. Now they pretty much know what everybody else is making and it's a comparison-type thing. Back then, everything was kept secret. Nobody knew what anybody was making. They never came out with the salaries. Sportswriters all tried to guess though.

"Quite a thrill": Pittsburgh Pirates jersey #9 is retired in 1987 as Milene, David, Darren and his wife Jill Mazeroski look on

My fondest memory of baseball is just being able to play it and make the big leagues. One of my biggest thrills was getting there and being able to stay there for seventeen years. Being known as a pretty good ballplayer. That's all I ever wanted. I had no big ideas. Just loved to play and would have played for nothing somewhere. If I hadn't played in the big leagues, I would have been playing for a bar, for beers and pizza. For the fun of it.

It's still a great game. I still enjoy going down with my son Darren, the head baseball coach at Gulf Coast Community College, and watching his players. I'll go down in the fall and watch them. They'll have the winter off and come back in the spring. I'll see how much they've improved after they work out for two or three months with good instruction and fundamentals. Darren does a great job teaching. They really do get better. I'm still in the game a little bit, in touch with baseball. My other son, David, didn't get into baseball. He graduated from Grove City College, went on to the University of Pittsburgh for his Masters degree, and is now a management consultant with Deloitte and Touche.

Everybody wonders about the money these days. I never got caught up in the money. I'd have played regardless. I would have been working in a coal mine or a steel mill somewhere, but I would have still played.

It was everything you'd want. A lot of people dream about doing what I did, just playing in the big leagues. I got to do it so I feel mighty fortunate. To have had a career in baseball, and then on top of that to hit a home run to win the World Series in the last of the ninth, like the little kids dream about, that's just icing on the cake. I lived a dream.

Having your number retired is quite a thrill, too. That's something that doesn't happen to ballplayers every day. The big names of Pittsburgh, Clemente and Pie Traynor, Honus Wagner, Stargell, that's big company there.

It's a funny thing about baseball. A football player who played in 1909 couldn't come back and play today — a 205-pound guard or tackle would have problems with a 310-pounder. A 6'2" center in basketball could not handle a 7'2" center of today. But in baseball, size doesn't rule.

And you know, in baseball, saving runs is still as important as producing runs. The object of the game is still to outscore your opponent. Over seventeen years, saving thousands of runs is like driving in thousands of runs. It's the same thing. You save one, you drive one in. So, what's the difference?

"I am one of the lucky people in the world"

Epilogue

I. HONORS

1. Eight Gold Glove Awards*

National League Second Basemen,
Gold Glove Winners, 1958-67

1958   **Bill Mazeroski**
1959   Charlie Neal, L.A.
1960   **Bill Mazeroski**
1961   **Bill Mazeroski**
1962   Kenny Hubbs, Chicago
1963   **Bill Mazeroski**
1964   **Bill Mazeroski**
1965   **Bill Mazeroski**
1966   **Bill Mazeroski**
1967   **Bill Mazeroski**

* Gold Glove selections made by major league players from 1958-1964, by managers and coaches since 1965.

2. Seven times selected for National League All-Star Team: 1958, 1959, 1960, 1962, 1963, 1964, 1967.

3. 1960 Sporting News Major League Player of The Year.

4. 1960 Babe Ruth Award (outstanding player in World Series).

II. RECORDS

NATIONAL LEAGUE RECORD

1. Years leading the league in total chances, second baseman, 8 (1958, 1960-'64, 1966-67).

MAJOR LEAGUE RECORDS

1. Games played in a season, second baseman, 163 (1967).
2. Years leading a league in assists, second baseman, 9 (1958, '60-'64, '66-'68).
3. Years leading a league in double plays, 8 (1960-'67).
4. Double plays, career, second baseman, 1706 (1956-'72).
5. Double plays, season, second baseman, 161 (1966).

DOUBLE PLAYS, SECOND BASEMAN

Career

1. **Bill Mazeroski**   **1706**
2. Nellie Fox   1619
3. Willie Randolph   1547
4. Bobby Doerr   1507
5. Joe Morgan   1505

Season

1. **Bill Mazeroski**   **1966** **161**
2. Jerry Priddy   1950 150
3. **Bill Mazeroski**   **1961** **144**
4. Nellie Fox   1957 141
   Dave Cash   1974 141
6. Buddy Myer   1935 138
   Bill Mazeroski   **1962** **138**
   Carlos Baerga   1992 138

III. BILL MAZEROSKI'S LIFETIME RECORD

YEAR	CLUB	G	AB	R	H	2B	3B	HR	RBI	BB	SO	AVG

Mazeroski, William Stanley "Maz" b: 9/5/36, Wheeling, West Virginia
BR/TR, 5'11.5", 183 lbs.
Major League Debut: July 7, 1956

YEAR	CLUB	G	AB	R	H	2B	3B	HR	RBI	BB	SO	AVG
1954	Wmsprt	93	315	35	74	6	8	3	28	25	41	.235
1955	Hwood	21	47	4	8	0	0	1	3	2	6	.170
	Wmsprt	114	413	68	121	13	7	11	65	40	34	.293
1956	Hwood	80	284	47	87	12	3	9	36	22	26	.306
	Pit-N	81	255	30	62	8	1	3	14	18	24	.243
1957	Pit-N	148	526	59	149	27	7	8	54	27	49	.283
1958	Pit-N	152	567	69	156	24	6	19	68	25	71	.275
1959	Pit-N	135	493	50	119	15	6	7	59	29	54	.241
1960	Pit-N	151	538	58	147	21	5	11	64	40	50	.273
1961	Pit-N	152	558	71	148	21	2	13	59	26	55	.265
1962	Pit-N	159	572	55	155	24	9	14	81	37	47	.271
1963	Pit-N	142	534	43	131	22	3	8	52	32	46	.245
1964	Pit-N	162	601	66	161	22	8	10	64	29	52	.268
1965	Pit-N	130	494	52	134	17	1	6	54	18	34	.271
1966	Pit-N	162	621	56	163	22	7	16	82	31	62	.262
1967	Pit-N	163	639	62	167	25	3	9	77	30	55	.261
1968	Pit-N	143	506	36	127	18	2	3	42	38	38	.251
1969	Pit-N	67	227	13	52	7	1	3	25	22	16	.229
1970	Pit-N	112	367	29	84	14	0	7	39	27	40	.229
1971	Pit-N	70	193	17	49	3	1	1	16	15	8	.254
1972	Pit-N	34	64	3	12	4	0	0	3	3	5	.188
Total	17	2163	7755	769	2016	294	62	138	853	447	706	.260

WORLD SERIES RECORD

Year	Club	G	AB	R	H	2B	3B	HR	RBI	AVG
1960	Pittsburgh	7	25	4	8	2	0	2	5	.320
1971	Pittsburgh	1	1	0	0	0	0	0	0	.000

LEAGUE CHAMPIONSHIP SERIES RECORD

Year	Club	G	AB	R	H	2B	3B	HR	RBI	AVG
1970	Pittsburgh	1	2	0	0	0	0	0	0	.000
1971	Pittsburgh	1	1	1	1	0	0	0	0	1.000
1972	Pittsburgh	2	2	0	1	0	0	0	0	.500

ALL-STAR GAME RECORD

Year	Club	G	AB	R	H	2B	3B	HR	RBI	AVG
1958	National	1	4	0	0	0	0	0	0	.000
1959	National*	1	1	0	1	0	0	0	1	1.000
1960	National**	2	4	0	1	0	0	0	1	.250
1962	National**	2	3	0	0	0	0	0	0	.000
1963	National	Named to team; replaced due to injury								
1964	National	Named to team; did not play								
1967	National	1	4	0	0	0	0	0	0	.000

* *Played in first game*
** *Played in both games*

IV. The 51 Other Regular
National League Second Basemen, 1957-1968

Bill Mazeroski averaged 149 games/year in this span. The National League played 154 games/year from 1957-1961, 162 games/year since.

1. **Brooklyn/L.A. Dodgers:**   Jim Gilliam, Charlie Neal, Larry Burright, Nate Oliver, Jim Lefebvre, Ron Hunt, Paul Popovich.

2. **Chicago Cubs:**   Bobby Morgan, Tony Taylor, Jerry Kindall, Don Zimmer, Kenny Hubbs, Joey Amalfitano, Glenn Beckert.

3. **Cincinnati Reds:**   Johnny Temple, Billy Martin, Don Blasingame, Pete Rose, Tommy Helms.

4. **Houston Colt .45s/Astros (1962-1968):**   Joey Amalfitano, Ernie Fazio, Nellie Fox, Joe Morgan, Denis Menke.

5. **Milwaukee/Atlanta Braves:**   Red Schoendienst, Felix Mantilla, Chuck Cottier, Frank Bolling, Woodie Woodward, Felix Millan.

6. **N.Y./San Francisco Giants:**   Danny O'Connell, Daryl Spencer, Don Blasingame, Joey Amalfitano, Chuck Hiller, Hal Lanier, Tito Fuentes, Ron Hunt.

7. N.Y. Mets (1962 to 1968): Charlie Neal, Ron Hunt,
Chuck Hiller, Jerry Buchek,
Phil Linz, Ken Boswell.

8. Philadelphia Phillies: Granny Hamner, Solly Hemus,
Sparky Anderson, Tony Taylor,
Cookie Rojas.

9. St. Louis Cardinals: Don Blasingame, Julian Javier

```
Dodgers . . . . . . . . . . . . . . 7
Cubs. . . . . . . . . . . . . . . . 7
Reds . . . . . . . . . . . . . . . . 5
Colt .45s/Astros . . . . . . . . 5
Braves. . . . . . . . . . . . . . . 6
Giants. . . . . . . . . . . . . . . 8
Mets. . . . . . . . . . . . . . . . 6
Phillies . . . . . . . . . . . . . . 5
St. Louis . . . . . . . . . . . . . 2
```

Total **51**

V. *Total Baseball* Rates Bill Mazeroski

Bill Mazeroski was a .260 lifetime hitter, slightly above average compared to second basemen playing in his era, 1956-1972. By any measure, his fielding was extraordinary.

Career fielding, in essence, the cumulative runs saved over seventeen years, has catapulted Mazeroski past many superior hitters when all players are rated according to their total contribution to a team -- fielding, hitting, pitching, and baserunning.

Pete Palmer is co-editor, with John Thorn, of *Total Baseball*, the official encyclopedia of major league baseball. Palmer's "Linear Weights" system attempts to evaluate any player at any position in any era, in terms of hitting, pitching, fielding, and baserunning, relative to an average ballplayer. "Fielding Runs" is Palmer's measure of a player's ability to exceed the league average in putouts, assists, double plays, and avoiding errors. Palmer's research indicates that Bill Mazeroski has recorded three of the top twenty-five seasons fielding (1963, 1962, and 1966).

FIELDING RUNS - SINGLE SEASON

1	Glenn Hubbard, 1985	61.8
2	Danny Richardson, 1892	57.6
3	**Bill Mazeroski, 1963**	**56.7**
4	Rabbit Maranville, 1914	51.8
5	Freddie Maguire, 1928	50.5
6	Nap Lajoie, 1908	49.3
7	Danny Richardson, 1891	49.1
8	Frankie Frisch, 1927	48.6
9	Hughie Critz, 1933	46.5
10	George Davis, 1899	46.3
11	Fred Pfeffer, 1884	45.5
12	Nap Lajoie, 1907	45.0
13	Dick Bartell, 1936	44.8
14	Ozzie Guillen, 1988	42.6
15	David Shean, 1910	42.5
	Lee Tannehill, 1911	42.5
17	Cupid Childs, 1896	42.4
18	Graig Nettles, 1971	42.3
19	Joe Gerhardt, 1890	41.5
20	Bid McPhee, 1889	41.1
	Bill Mazeroski, 1962	**41.1**
	Ryne Sandberg, 1983	41.1
23	Harlond Clift, 1937	41.0
	Glenn Hubbard, 1986	41.0
25	**Bill Mazeroski, 1966**	**40.8**
	Ozzie Smith, 1980	40.8

FIELDING RUNS - LIFETIME (All Positions)

1	Nap Lajoie	.367
2	**Bill Mazeroski**	**.362**
3	Bill Dahlen	.348
4	Bid McPhee	.314
5	Fred Pfeffer	.266
6	Mike Schmidt	.265
7	George Davis	.249
8	Tris Speaker	.248
9	Jack Glasscock	.240
10	Ozzie Smith	236 *

*Does not include 1995

FIELDING RUNS - LIFETIME (Second Base)

1	Nap Lajoie	.368
2	**Bill Mazeroski**	**.363**
3	Bid McPhee	.314
4	Fred Pfeffer	.257
5	Glenn Hubbard	.229
6	Bobby Doerr	.180
7	Joe Gerhardt	.160
8	Lou Bierbauer	.153
9	Bobby Knoop	.150
10	Ski Melillo	.148

Palmer's formula for "Fielding Wins" is based on the league average of Runs needed to produce a Win; this is a persuasive measure of Mazeroski's dominance in the field among all players:

FIELDING WINS - LIFETIME (All Positions)

1	**Bill Mazeroski**	**. 37.7**
2	Nap Lajoie	. . . . .37.6
3	Bill Dahlen	. . . . .33.1
4	Mike Schmidt	. . . . . .27.7
5	Bid McPhee	. . . . .27.3
6	Tris Speaker	. . . . .25.3
7	Ozzie Smith	. . . . . . .24.6
8	Clete Boyer	. . . . .24.2
9	Glenn Hubbard	. . . . . .23.8
10	George Davis	. . . . . .23.4

Palmer's total ranking (hitting, pitching, fielding, baserunning) of every player (excludes Negro League players whose exploits were not recorded in sufficient detail to make statistical comparisons):

TOTAL BASEBALL RANKING - LIFETIME
(Boldfaced players are not in Hall of Fame as of January, 1996)

1	Babe Ruth	124.7
2	Nap Lajoie	94.3
3	Willie Mays	92.2
4	Ty Cobb	91.2
5	Walter Johnson	90.1
6	Hank Aaron	89.8
7	Tris Speaker	86.5
8	Ted Williams	85.7
9	Honus Wagner	81.3
10	Rogers Hornsby	81.1
11	Cy Young	79.9
12	Mike Schmidt	78.4
13	Mickey Mantle	76.1
14	**Rickey Henderson**	**74.6** *
15	Stan Musial	70.5
16	Eddie Collins	69.7
17	Frank Robinson	69.0
18	Lou Gehrig	65.7
19	Pete Alexander	64.9
20	Christy Mathewson	62.7
	Mel Ott	62.7
22	Lefty Grove	61.2
23	Kid Nichols	60.9
24	Joe Morgan	56.3
25	Jimmie Foxx	54.3
26	Eddie Mathews	51.6
27	**Bill Dahlen**	**51.4**
28	**Tim Raines**	**51.0** *
29	**George Davis**	**50.0**
30	**Barry Bonds**	**49.4** *
31	John Clarkson	48.7
32	Tom Seaver	48.2
33	Warren Spahn	47.0
34	Joe DiMaggio	46.9
35	Carl Yastrzemski	45.5
36	Al Kaline	44.6